CLASSICS & CREATIONS

Classics & Creations

a world of vegetarian cooking

SAWAN KIRPAL PUBLICATIONS

Editor
Arlene Muska

Associate Editors
Ruth Seader
Sheila Grayson
Sandy Glassman
Janice Grossberg

Illustrations
Valerie Poole

Graphic Design
George Barham

Typography
Ajili Hodari

Published by Sawan Kirpal Publications,
Bowling Green, Virginia 22427, and
2 Canal Road, Vijay Nagar, Delhi-110009, India

First Printing: 1985

ISBN 0-918224-19-5

Library of Congress Catalog Number: 84-052832

Printed in the United States of America

Acknowledgements

To all of you from the States and abroad who helped in so many ways, I thank you. This cookbook would not have been possible without you, and I am grateful to you all.

Ellen Anderson
Rus Anderson
Sarah and Thomas Andryuk
Ellen Angus
Bill Arnold
Andrea Aschenbreuner
Sharon Ashley
Laura Baugh
Pat Beazley
Valerie Beazley
Bonnie Bednarik
Mary Grace Berger
Brigette Boehm
Helene Broska
Laura Buck
Nora Buck
Sandra Cardenas
Francine Cataldo
Kay Cataldo
Laura Clark
Cindy Delaney
Amie Densmire
Jane Disinger
Elizabeth Dodge
Olga Donenberg
Pam Dorsey
Leslie Dosa
Raji Duggal
Joan Eskow
Lorrie Fitzsimmons
Lee Frisch
Ruth Ann Fulton
Doe Gardiner
Maurie Goldberg
Stephanie Goldreyer
Irene Gregory
Dr. Ted Greiner
Diane Gresalti

Kathy Grinold
Birute Guides
Winda Guth
Lisa Ham
Marilyn Handel
Pam Hanlon
Norm and Roz Hassinger
Bette Hoffman
Karen Holm
Nancy Hribar
Conni Isensee
Marv and Michele Jonesi
Jan Jorrin
Jane Kaiser
Sally Kauffmann
Bill Klempt
Surinder Kochar
Kathryn Kruger
Catherine Lasley
Ricki Linksman
Shirley Lohnes
Fay March
Tricia Maynard
Doreen McCandess
Katie McCluney
Nancy McClure
Miriam Meppelink
Willi and Ingrid Michael
Adeline Minogue
Pat Moed
Cathy Muska
Debbie Muska
James Nicholson
Gisela Ohlrich
Joyce Owen
Diane Paquette
Sarah Paquette
Ellen Perkins

Esther Piner
Maureen Pletcher
Elinor Pollack
Suzanne Polvin
Audrey Post
Martin and Margorie Postal
Debbie Purdy
Geeta Ravens
Mary Robbins
Wayne Sabbak
Penny Sandusky
Tina Saposnik
Bette Drew Sarinsky
Ellen Seader
Joan Seader
Karen Seader
Dr. Vinod Sena
Gayle Shaffer
Dr. Joel and Ileane Shepperd
Cathy Sherry
George and Sharon Shively
Karen Silverman
Marie Smith
Martha Smith
Susanne Smith
Phillip and Doone Squire
Dr. Art Stein
Lucille Summers
Mira and Neil Tessler
Bonnie Tipton
Francine Toupin
Angie Turkfeld
Clare Vidich
Dr. Virginia Vidich
Mari Walden
Shelley Williams
Bruno Zaffina
Nina Zaslove
Diane Zeroll

Dedicated
to Sant Darshan Singh
whose reverence for life
and love for all creation
was the inspiration for
this cookbook

Contents

Introduction

Dear Readers,

It is with great pleasure that we present *Classics & Creations*. This international repertoire of both simple and challenging recipes will be a collection you can rely upon for nutritious and satisfying meals.

Classics & Creations is the first of two volumes. Here you will find a wide selection of tasty appetizers and hors d'oeuvres, beverages and non-alcoholic cocktails, protein-rich burgers and delicious sandwich fillings. This volume features unique eggless quiches, souffles and even omelets. Also included are hearty breads and rolls, and a wide range of soups and salads.

The recipes in this book have been collected and developed over the past several years. My own interest in vegetarian cooking began in 1977 when a physician recommended the diet to improve our family's health. My transition to vegetarianism was gradual, and it was during this period that I started becoming sensitive to the ethical aspects of the vegetarian diet. With increased self-introspection, a new consciousness started to awaken within me, and I felt myself becoming more and more alive spiritually. At this time, I was led to my spiritual teacher, Sant Darshan Singh. It was he who introduced me to the art of "inner nourishment" through meditation, and his impact on my life has been tremendous.

Because of an increasing commitment to a lacto-vegetarian diet, I began conducting vegetarian cooking classes in my home near Chicago in addition to my work as an artist and art teacher. It was in 1979, while studying Surat Shabd Yoga with Sant Darshan Singh at Kirpal Ashram in Delhi, India, that he suggested I begin working on a cookbook. With the co-operation of my husband, Ed, and sons, Brad and Todd, I began the effort wholeheartedly.

As the months went on, many talented people from all over the country offered their help. However, throughout this project, my associate editors, Ruth Seader, Sheila Grayson, Sandra Glassman and Janice Grossberg, have been my partners. They worked long hours on each phase of the book and participated in all aspects of its development. I also continuously received much needed encouragement from Sant Darshan Singh as well as from his dear wife, Harbhajan Kaur; and it was their daughter-in-law, Rita Duggal, who aided with the Western adaptations of the Indian recipes in this and the forthcoming companion volume.

I hope you will enjoy these recipes as much as we have: the classics, the ethnic recipes handed down for generations, the adaptations from the mainstream of the American diet together with our own creations.

As a final note, I would like to suggest that the most important ingredient in any recipe is the practice of cooking in a calm atmosphere with love in our hearts and God on our minds. If we then offer our sincere thanks for the food we are about to eat, it will provide nourishment, in both body and spirit, to all who share it.

Arlene Muska
Chicago 1985

The Vegetarian Way of Life

Science is beginning to arrive at the conclusions reached by the saints and mystics from the earliest times. Thus, in the realm of nutrition, modern research is confirming the supremacy of the vegetarian diet which has been advocated by those leading a spiritual life. In all respects — physical, moral, and spiritual — the vegetarian diet is the most suitable for man.

Many great philosophers, artists, poets, writers, and some of the most enlightened monarchs have been vegetarians. Ashoka the Great, Emperor Akbar, Sir Isaac Newton, Percy Bysshe Shelley, Leo Tolstoy, Mahatma Gandhi, and Albert Schweitzer are just a few examples. It was their sensitivity and compassion which led them to adopt the path of nonviolence towards all creation. There is an interesting anecdote from the life of George Bernard Shaw regarding the vegetarian diet. Once when he was very ill, the doctors said that unless he started eating eggs and taking meat soup, he would die. As he was a strict vegetarian, he refused to follow the doctors' orders. When the doctors stuck to their point of view and told him they could not guarantee that he would survive the illness, G.B. Shaw called for his private secretary and, in the presence of the doctors, dictated his will. It said, "I solemnly declare that it is my last wish that when I am no longer a captive of this physical body, my coffin, when carried to the graveyard, be accompanied by mourners of the following categories: first, birds; second, sheep, lambs, and cows, and other animals of the kind; third, live fish in an aquarium. Each of these mourners should carry a placard bearing the inscription: 'O Lord, be gracious to our benefactor G.B. Shaw who gave his life for saving others!'"

Leonardo da Vinci, another vegetarian, had great compassion. If he saw a caged bird, he would pay the owner for the cage and the bird. Then he would open the cage door and watch the joyful bird soar to freedom.

God has provided man with an abundance of fruits, nuts, vegetables, grains, legumes, and herbs for food. In addition, we can eat dairy products, which do not require killing animals. It is true that to live in this world, we must destroy some life; even the plants we eat and the bacteria we breathe have life. The law of karma — every action has a reaction — operates in the realm of diet as it does in all other spheres of life. So the saints say that since we cannot do without food, we should choose that diet which causes the least possible pain, the least possible sin. An incident which I recollect will explain this rather well. Sant Kirpal Singh was in spiritual retreat in Rishikesh for several months in 1948. I spent some weeks with him. Our way of life was extremely simple there, and we used large leaves as plates for our food. One day after I plucked the leaves for the evening meal, the Beloved Master asked me to count them. They were somewhat in excess of the number of people who were to have their food. He told me that in the future I should be more careful and count the number in our group beforehand. He said, "You have taken off two more leaves than were needed. They too have life."

While science teaches that all matter is composed of various combinations of chemical elements of the periodic table, the ancient scriptures of the East introduce a further dimension. They tell of a life force within the various life forms — man, animal, bird, reptile, and plant. The least life force is found in the plants. To explain this, the scriptures speak of five creative and component qualities which are: water, earth, fire, air, and ether. Man's body is said to contain all five qualities, and he is considered to be the highest and most valued in this creation. The killing of one's fellow man is regarded as the most heinous crime and through the ages has been punishable by death. The next in value are the quadrupeds and beasts which have four qualities, with ether being absent or forming a negligible portion. According to most laws, the killing of an animal usually entails a penalty equal to the price of the animal in question. The third category includes birds which have three active qualities in them — water, fire, and air. If someone kills a stray bird, he usually goes scot-free, and if a "protected" bird is killed the hunter may have to pay a small penalty for it. Lesser still is the value of reptiles, worms, and insects which have only two active qualities —

earth and fire, as the other three qualities exist in a dormant form. The death of these species of life does not involve any penalty according to most of the laws in this world. The least value is placed on roots, vegetables, and fruits which contain only the quality of water in an active state. Thus, ethically speaking, the vegetarian or fruitarian diet is the least pain producing, and by adopting it, man contracts the least karmic debt. Sarmad, a seventeenth century Sufi of Jewish origin, expressed the same truth in the simplest of words: "The Light of Life, which is the Lord, is dormant in the mineral world, is in the dream-state in the vegetable world, awakens in the animal world, and comes to full consciousness in man."

A similar perspective may be found in the writings of our modern spiritual and philosophical thinkers. Teilhard de Chardin, for example, has noted in *The Phenomenon of Man* that there are differing degrees of consciousness in living organisms, depending upon their complexity. He argues that consciousness becomes more perfected and recognizable in richer, more complex, and more original life forms — the highest being man himself. This view would produce essentially the same dietary guidelines as do the teachings of the ancient scriptures. Recognizing the need to keep our bodies going while keeping in view the goal of nonviolence, we would wish to follow the vegetarian diet because it results in the least possible destruction.

Many people have misunderstandings about the nutritional value of the vegetarian diet, and they think it does not give us the proper food value. The main complaint against the vegetarian diet has been that it does not provide the essential proteins. But the latest research confirms that a balanced vegetarian diet definitely gives more than enough protein, as well as the required vitamins, minerals, and calories. I have been in touch with leading nutritionists, and their evidence shows that a vegetarian diet can certainly give us all the necessary nutrients. In fact, the United States Food and Drug Administration's periodical "FDA Consumer" lauds the efficacy and practicality of the vegetarian diet. It points out that as a result of a 1974 report by the Food Nutrition Board of the National Academy of Sciences, "The idea that vegetarians can't get what their bodies need without meat was pretty well put into the myth category." Moreover, by abstaining from alcohol and drugs which deplete the body of valuable nutrients, vegetarians are able to maintain health and assimilate higher levels of vitamins and minerals as compared with those who partake of alcohol, drugs, and animal foods. As more and more research is conducted, scientists, biologists, and nutritionists are finding that the vegetarian diet is most wholesome and healthful for man.

The strongest animals with the greatest endurance are vegetarians. The elephant, the ox, and the horse are known for their might and capacity to work. We even measure the power of engines in "horsepower." And, to refute any claims that vegetarianism may not support the highest intellectual development, we have already mentioned that many of our greatest, most creative thinkers have been vegetarians.

Even from the physiological point of view, man is most suited to a vegetarian diet — his physical structure does not place him in the same category as meat-eating animals. For example, carnivorous animals have big cuspids, or canine teeth, as well as claws for ripping and tearing flesh; man does not. Man's teeth more closely resemble the herbivorous animals which have special flat molars for grinding. Further, the intestines of meat-eating animals are short (about three times the length of the trunk of their body) so that the flesh is absorbed or expelled before it putrefies and produces poisons. But man and the herbivorous animals have very long intestines (about ten to twelve times the length of the trunk of their body).

Should we stop to think about it, we would realize that the food we eat has an effect on our physical, emotional, and mental makeup. If we are trying to lead a life of nonviolence and compassion, if we are trying to become more serene and peaceful, if we are trying to control our mind and senses, then we will naturally want to follow a diet that helps us achieve our goal. There is a beautiful story related by Attar about the great Sufi lady saint Rabia Basri. Once when she had gone to the mountains, a band of wild creatures — deer and gazelle and mountain goats and wild asses — gathered around her. They came and looked at her and drew close to her. Suddenly, Hasan-al-Basri arrived on the scene, and when he saw Rabia he approached her. The wild creatures, when they saw Hasan, all fled in terror. Hasan was vexed when he saw this. He looked at Rabia and asked, "Why did they run away in fear from me while they were friendly to you?" Rabia asked, "What have you eaten today?" He said, "Some onion fried in fat." She said, "You eat of their fat; why should they not flee from you?"

If we become sensitive to what we eat, our very way of life will be affected. When the Roman poet Seneca, on learning of the teachings of Pythagoras, became a vegetarian, he found the change a happy one and discovered to his surprise that his "mind had grown more alert and more enlightened."

In terms of socio-economics too, vegetarianism is the most practical diet. It takes ten acres of pasture land to produce a certain amount of meat protein, but the same amount of vegetable protein can be produced on only one acre of land. So nine acres of land are wasted when meat is produced. Similarly, an animal eats sixteen pounds of grain to produce only one pound of meat, and thus fifteen pounds of grain are wasted. God has given us the facilities and bounties of nature by which all His children can be fed. Vegetarianism is much more productive and much less wasteful. So in this regard too, the vegetarian diet is the most rational.

When a predator preys on another creature, he does so for his own survival; he has no other means of sustaining life. But when a man turns non-vegetarian, he can plead no such compulsion. In fact, his desire to give up the way of life natural to his species is highly wasteful and morally indefensible. If those who partake of meat were to witness the manner in which it is "manufactured" in the slaughterhouse, many of them would give it up in revulsion.

Food can be categorized according to the effect it has upon man. In India, three broad categories of diet have been given: pure (satvik) foods, energizing (rajsik) foods, and stupefying (tamsik) foods. Pure foods include vegetables, grains, beans and other legumes, fruits and nuts, as well as milk, butter, and cheese in moderation. This diet produces serenity and equipoise, and it is said to keep one free from all types of impurities. The energizing foods include pepper, spices, condiments, and sour and bitter things. Foods of this type act as stimulants, and excite the senses. Stupefying foods include stale foods, meat, fish, fowl and eggs, and alcoholic beverages — such a diet produces inertia. I am often asked about the rationale of not taking even infertile eggs, which some people label as "vegetarian eggs." Apart from the fact that such an egg represents a form of life which cannot fulfill itself, it has the same undesirable effect on us as a fertile egg. It stupefies the mind and enflames the passions. Taking these factors into view, the saints and sages from time immemorial have followed the pure diet because it is most helpful for spiritual advancement.

For those who wish to follow the path leading to self-knowledge and God-realization, a strict vegetarian diet is essential. If we examine various religious and mystic traditions, we find that they recommend or require vegetarianism. Pythagoras and his followers were strict vegetarians. The Greek sage taught: "My friends, do not defile your bodies by partaking of impure foods. We have enough of grains and trees which are loaded with fruits. We have delicious vegetables and roots which can be readily cooked. And there is no dearth of milk and honey. Our earth has an abundance of such pure and harmless foods and there is no need for us to partake of meals for which blood has to be shed and innocent life sacrificed."

Many of the famous early philosophers such as Plato, Plotinus, Empedocles, Appolonius, Plutarch, and Porphyry also followed the vegetarian diet. Again, many of the early mystery religions, such as the Orphics and the Essenes, had vegetarianism as a prerequisite for initiation. If we study the Holy Bible we find that in Genesis, God says, "I have given you every herb bearing seed which is upon the face of all the earth, and every tree, in which is the fruit of a tree yielding seed; to you it shall be for meat." Even when God gave Moses the Ten Commandments, vegetarianism was necessarily implied. If we follow the commandment, "Thou shalt not kill," it is naturally out of the question to eat meat, fish, fowl, or eggs. How can we claim to be lovers of God, lovers of His creation, if we kill the humbler members of God's family?

Jesus Christ was the Apostle of Peace; he was the embodiment of nonviolence. He taught, "Whosoever shall smite thee on thy right cheek, turn to him the other also." If he was nonviolent to that extent, could he have been violent to the lower rungs of God's creation? Christ taught universal love and total nonviolence. He commanded that we have love for all.

The great Sufi saints of the past were vegetarians. Thus, Mirdad declares, "Those who follow the spiritual path must never forget that if they partake of flesh, they must pay for it with their own flesh." Buddha, the Compassionate One, taught nonviolence towards all creatures, and originally his followers were vegetarians. Mahavira, the founder of the Jain religion, preached a strict vegetarian diet. And, of course, vegetarianism is an integral part of the Hindu religious tradition. At Sikh gurdwaras (temples) no meat is served in the free kitchen, and when the Sikhs observe a religious ceremony in their homes, vegetarian meals are served after the recitation of the scriptures. A Mughal historian significantly has recorded in his book *Dabistan-e-Mazahib* (School of Religions) that Guru Arjan Dev made a special proclamation: "Eating of meat is forbidden among those who follow Guru Nanak." Instructions to disciples given by Guru Har Gobind, the Sixth Sikh Guru, are quite explicit: "Do not go near fish and meat."*

If you make a comparative study of religious traditions, you will find that after a saint or a Master has concluded his ministry, the esoteric side of his teachings is rapidly forgotten and is replaced by rites and rituals. To make the teachings more acceptable to a large number of people, changes are often made in diet and discipline by those who come after him. But the mystic tradition is clear in advocating vegetarianism.

In addition to being careful about what type of food we eat, we should also be careful about how much we eat. The basic principle with regard to food is, "Eat to live, not live to eat." Unfortunately, most of us live to eat — and overeat. When we are given a new or delicious dish, we overeat. And sometimes to show someone we appreciate their hospitality, we overeat. But overeating is the cause of many of our health problems, and some of our meditation problems as well. The Persian mystic Sheikh Saadi has said that because we are filled up to our noses with food, we are not able to see the Light of God. He advised that the stomach be divided into four compartments: two for filling with simple food; one for water; while reserving one for the Light of God.

There is an instructive incident from the life of Prophet Mohammed. One day, a physician came to him and offered his services for the sick and ailing in the Umat, the Prophet's following. He remained idle for six months as none of the Prophet's followers fell ill. He approached the Prophet and asked for permission to leave, as no one there required his services. Hazrat Mohammed, with a gentle smile on his lips, bid good-bye to the physician saying that so long as the congregation lived by his instructions, they would not fall sick: Always eat a little less than what one may, in his hunger, otherwise like to take.

If we eat too much we feel sleepy and drowsy, and for those on the spiritual path, more time spent sleeping means less time for meditation. And even when we do meditate, if we overeat we may be drowsy. Once a man went to a saint and complained, "Sir, my meditations are not good." The saint replied, "Look to your stomach." Another man came to this saint and said, "I cannot control my mind." The saint replied, "Look to your stomach." A third man came and said, "I am not having good health." And the saint again replied, "Look to your stomach." So eating less than we have an appetite for is good not only for our meditations but also for our health.

I often come across people for whom the question "What is the natural diet for man?" has become such an obsession that they lose sight of the larger humane and spiritual purposes which the vegetarian diet fulfills. Vegetarianism is not an end in itself, but an indispensable means to an end. Rightly understood, we should see diet not as something separate, but as an integral part of a whole philosophy, a whole way of life.

Albert Einstein, the great physicist, was so convinced of the far-reaching impact which the vegetarian way of life can have on our nature that he believed, if adopted universally, it would lead to great improvement in the human condition. If we wish to follow the path of nonviolence and love for all creation, then we will adhere to a strict vegetarian diet. In doing so, we will not only have compassion on the younger members of God's creation, and on our fellow man, but we will also have compassion on our own selves.

Darshan Singh

*These instructions, sent out in a circular called "Hukamnama," are preserved at Patna Sahib Gurdwara.

Appetizers

Cauliflower Cocktail

A low-calorie, delightfully refreshing appetizer.

1   medium-sized cauliflower, cut
    into flowerets
    Lettuce leaves
1   large lemon, cut into thin wedges

Cocktail Sauce:
¾   cup ketchup or chili sauce
2   to 4 tablespoons prepared white
    horseradish
2   tablespoons fresh lemon juice

● Place flowerets in a saucepan with ½-inch of lightly salted water. Bring to a boil. Reduce heat and cook covered for 3 to 5 minutes until just tender-crisp. ● Remove from heat and drain. Plunge cauliflower into a large bowl of cold water to stop cooking process. Drain, then chill. ● To serve, line a platter with lettuce leaves and place lemon wedges around edge. ● Combine Cocktail Sauce ingredients. Place in a bowl in the center of platter. Arrange chilled cauliflower around the bowl. Squeeze one or two wedges of lemon into the sauce.

Note: Prepared cocktail sauce may be purchased in the ketchup section of most grocery stores.

Yield: 6 to 8 servings

Stuffed Fresh Mushrooms

Mushroom lovers will appreciate the woodsy flavor of these cheese-filled raw mushrooms.

24   large fresh mushrooms
    Lemon juice
1   8-ounce package cream cheese, at
    room temperature
2   tablespoons butter, at room
    temperature
1   tablespoon chopped fresh parsley
1   tablespoon chopped fresh chives
1   teaspoon minced fresh basil or
    ½ teaspoon crumbled dry

1   tablespoon minced fresh onion
1   teaspoon prepared mustard
½   teaspoon caraway seeds
4   teaspoons whole capers
    Salt and pepper to taste
Garnish:
    Paprika
    Sliced black olives
    Halved small cherry tomatoes

● Carve stems out of each mushroom and reserve stems for another use. To clean mushrooms, wipe with a damp cloth (do not place under running water). Sprinkle with lemon juice to prevent discoloration and set on paper towels to dry. ● Combine cream cheese, butter, parsley, chives, basil, onion, mustard and caraway seeds. Beat until light and fluffy. Stir in capers by hand, then add salt and pepper. ● Fill mushrooms with cream cheese mixture. Sprinkle top with paprika. Add additional parsley or chopped fresh chives to top if desired. Garnish with a slice of olive or halved cherry tomato. Serve chilled.

Variation: Use filling to stuff tomatoes instead of mushrooms. Select large cherry tomatoes, hollow out centers with a serrated knife and fill with cream cheese mixture.

Note: After chilling stuffed mushrooms, they can also be sliced and served on crackers.

Yield: 2 dozen mushrooms

Baked Stuffed Mushrooms

Large sizzling-hot mushrooms, mounded high with our savory filling.

24 large fresh mushrooms	¼ teaspoon paprika
8 tablespoons butter	Salt and pepper to taste
2 medium-sized onions, finely chopped	¾ cup or more bread crumbs
¼ teaspoon garlic powder	½ cup shredded mozzarella
½ teaspoon crumbled dry basil	cheese (optional)
½ teaspoon crumbled dry oregano	

● Clean mushrooms well and place on paper towels. Remove stems and carve out a portion of the center of each mushroom. Finely chop stems and carvings and set aside. ● In a large skillet, sauté mushroom caps for 2 to 4 minutes in 2 tablespoons of the butter. Remove caps and place on a greased baking sheet, hollow side up. In the same skillet, brown onions on high heat for a few minutes, stirring constantly. Add remaining 6 tablespoons of butter. Sauté onions over medium-low heat for 5 minutes. ● Add chopped mushrooms and seasonings. Cook 5 more minutes. Stir in bread crumbs and cheese. ● Fill mushroom caps with stuffing. Place under broiler for 5 minutes or until nicely browned. Serve hot.

Yield: 2 dozen

Caponata

This robust Italian salad is equally enjoyable as an appetizer, a sandwich topping or part of an antipasto.

1 large eggplant	¼ teaspoon black pepper
⅔ cup vegetable oil (3 tablespoons of which is olive oil)	½ teaspoon crumbled dry basil
	½ teaspoon crumbled dry oregano
2 cups finely chopped Spanish onion	1½ teaspoons salt
1 large green bell pepper, cut into 1-inch squares	Pinch of cayenne pepper
	1 tablespoon mild-flavored honey
1 cup finely chopped celery	1 tablespoon chopped walnuts or pine
1 16-ounce can tomatoes, drained and chopped	nuts (optional)
	½ cup pitted black or green olives
¼ cup apple cider vinegar	¼ cup capers with some of the juice

● Cut unpeeled eggplant into 1-inch cubes (see note). Sprinkle lightly with salt and leave for ½ hour. Rinse under running water and pat dry. ● In a large skillet, sauté eggplant in ⅓ cup of the mixed oil for 5 minutes. Remove to a bowl. Add remaining ⅓ cup oil to the skillet. Sauté onion in oil for about 10 minutes. Add green pepper, celery, and tomatoes. Cook over medium heat for 15 minutes, stirring occasionally. ● Add vinegar, seasonings, honey, chopped walnuts or pine nuts, and eggplant. Cover and simmer for 15 minutes. Stir in olives and capers. ● Place in a bowl and cover. Chill well.

Note: For use as a dip, chop eggplant and green pepper into smaller pieces when preparing.

Yield: 1 quart

Puff Pastry Pinwheels

Delicate, flaky puff pastry combines well with the nutty flavor of soybeans in this attractive and nutritious hors d'oeuvre.

1⅓ cups cooked soybeans (1 15-ounce can, drained)
2 tablespoons vegetable oil
1 tablespoon tamari

2 tablespoons ketchup
1 sheet frozen puff pastry, thawed according to package instructions
6 thin slices Swiss cheese (about 4 × 6 inches), at room temperature

● Place soybeans, vegetable oil, tamari and ketchup in a food processor and blend until just slightly textured (or mash by hand). ● Open puff pastry sheet and lay flat. Cut along folds to make three pieces. Cut each of these crosswise, in half. Roll out to make six 5 × 7-inch rectangles. ● Divide soybean filling between the six sheets (about ⅓ cup each). Spread over pastry, leaving ½-inch border around all edges. Lay one slice of Swiss cheese over filling. Moisten edges of the pastry with water. Roll up into a jelly-roll shape, starting with the 5-inch edge. Pinch seams and edges to seal. ● Cover each roll separately with plastic wrap or waxed paper. Chill for at least 2 hours until firm. ● Remove from refrigerator and slice each roll crosswise into six equal rounds. Place on greased baking sheets, arranging end pieces seam-side down. Bake at 425° F. for 7 to 10 minutes. Serve hot or at room temperature.

Yield: 3 dozen

Barbecued Tofu Strips

The sweet and pungent sauce bakes deeply into the tofu strips, creating a delectable appetizer.

8 ounces firm tofu, pressed
¼ cup tamari

¼ cup vegetable oil
Sweet and sour sauce

● Cut pressed tofu into ¼-inch slices. Place in a single layer in a small pan and pour tamari over strips. Marinate in tamari for 15 to 60 minutes, turning occasionally to coat evenly. The longer the marination time, the stronger the tamari flavor. Drain. ● Heat vegetable oil in a skillet and fry tofu on both sides until lightly browned. Dip fried tofu slices in a bowl of sweet and sour sauce to coat both sides. Lay strips in a single layer in a heavy baking pan or casserole dish. ● Bake at 400° F. on the lowest oven rack for 20 minutes. Flip strips with a spatula and bake an additional 10 to 15 minutes until the sauce is well baked in. ● Serve hot with extra sweet and sour sauce on the side for dipping.

Yield: 1 dozen

Fancy Franks

An easy and fanciful way to serve this popular hors d'oeuvre.

8   vegetarian hot dogs
½   cup ketchup

2   cups (or more) wheat or corn flakes, coarsely crushed
    Prepared mustard

● Cut vegetarian hot dogs crosswise into thirds. Dip in ketchup and coat well. Roll in crushed flakes, adding more if needed. Place on a lightly greased baking sheet. ● Bake at 350° F. for 15 minutes. Serve hot with a bowl of mustard for dipping.

Note: Crush flakes in a blender or food processor, or pour into a plastic bag and crush with hands on a flat surface.

Yield: 2 dozen

Vegetarian Gefullte Fish

Indulge in the nostalgia of this ethnic treat. Looks like traditional gefullte fish but has its own unique flavor.

2   small onions, diced
2   tablespoons vegetable oil
1   medium-sized cauliflower, coarsely chopped
2   tablespoons water
½   cup cream cheese, at room temperature

⅓   cup matzo meal
2   teaspoons Cocktail Sauce
    Salt to taste
    Dash of white pepper
Garnish:
    Sliced, cooked carrots
    Prepared white horseradish

● In a large skillet, sauté onions in vegetable oil for 5 to 10 minutes. Do not allow onions to brown. ● Add cauliflower and 2 tablespoons water. Cover and cook over medium-low heat for 20 to 30 minutes or until cauliflower is tender. Stir occasionally, adding 1 or 2 more tablespoons water if necessary. Drain any excess liquid at end of cooking time. ● Run cauliflower and onions through a food mill or mash in a bowl leaving mixture slightly textured. Let cool for 10 minutes. Mix thoroughly with cream cheese, matzo meal, Cocktail Sauce, salt and pepper. ● Form into the traditional shape of oval patties, about 4 × 2 × 1½ inches. Refrigerate for several hours. ● Garnish with carrots and serve cold with horseradish.

Yield: 6 to 8 servings

Vegetarian Lox

Eggplant has many guises, and this one is a remarkable taste-alike of smoked salmon (lox).

1	medium-sized eggplant	2	tablespoons water
	Salt for sprinkling	½	teaspoon sugar
⅓	cup vegetable oil	¼	teaspoon salt (optional)
2	teaspoons white vinegar	8	drops natural red food color
¼	to ½ teaspoon liquid hickory smoke concentrate	2	drops natural yellow food color

● Peel eggplant and slice into 3 × 1¼ × ¼-inch strips. Place eggplant on a rimmed platter and sprinkle generously with salt. Cover with a paper towel or clean cloth. Press with a weight (such as a pot filled with water) for several hours or overnight. Drain. ● Fry eggplant in vegetable oil over low heat without allowing slices to brown. Eggplant should become soft but not mushy. ● In a small bowl combine vinegar, hickory smoke concentrate, water, sugar, salt to taste and food color. Stir this mixture into eggplant, tossing slices to coat evenly. Cook for 2 minutes. Drain eggplant strips well on paper towels and let cool. ● Serve on split bagels with cream cheese. Also good on small party rye or pumpernickle bread with cream cheese and chopped onion.

Yield: about 2 cups

Vegetarian Pickled Herring

You will find great taste and texture in these eggplant "filets" marinated in a tangy cream sauce with onions.

1	medium-sized eggplant	1	cup dairy sour cream
	Salt for sprinkling	1	tablespoon lemon juice
⅓	cup vegetable oil	2	tablespoons milk or buttermilk
2	tablespoons white vinegar	½	large sweet Spanish onion, thinly sliced
1	teaspoon sugar		

● Peel eggplant and slice into 3 × 1¼ × ¼-inch strips. Place eggplant on a rimmed platter and sprinkle generously with salt. Cover with a paper towel or clean cloth. Press with a weight (such as a pot filled with water) for several hours or overnight. Drain. ● Fry eggplant in vegetable oil over low heat until tender. Add vinegar and ½ teaspoon of the sugar. Cook 1 more minute. Drain on paper towels. ● Combine remaining ½ teaspoon sugar with sour cream, lemon juice, milk or buttermilk, and onion in a bowl. Stir to mix. Add eggplant and toss to coat well. Cover and refrigerate before serving.

Yield: about 3 cups

Party Cheese Ball

A perennial favorite with cream cheese, sweet pineapple and crunchy nuts.

2   cups chopped walnuts
2   8-ounce packages cream cheese, at
      room temperature
½ large green bell pepper, finely
      chopped

1   7-ounce can crushed pineapple,
      drained
1   tablespoon dry onion flakes
2   teaspoons powdered vegetable seasoning
      Salt to taste

● Set aside ¾ cup of chopped walnuts. Combine all remaining ingredients in a bowl and mix thoroughly. Form into a ball. Roll in reserved walnuts. ● Cover with plastic wrap and refrigerate until firm. Serve on a plate and surround with crackers.

Yield: 16 servings

Cheese Shorties

Try these melt-in-your-mouth shorties at your next party.

1   pound sharp Cheddar cheese, shredded
1   cup butter, at room temperature
½ teaspoon garlic salt (optional)

2   cups unbleached white flour, sifted
      Paprika
      Grated Parmesan cheese

● Combine cheese, butter and garlic salt. Add flour and mix well with hands. Shape into 4 long rolls, 1 inch in diameter. Wrap each roll in wax paper or plastic wrap and refrigerate until firm (or freeze). ● Remove from refrigerator. *(If frozen, defrost in refrigerator before using.)* Slice each roll into 12 equal rounds. Place 1 inch apart on ungreased baking sheets and garnish with a sprinkle of paprika and Parmesan cheese. ● Bake at 400° F. for about 10 minutes until golden. Remove from baking sheets to cool. Serve at room temperature.

Note: This dough can be made in advance and kept in refrigerator for up to 2 weeks or in freezer for 2 months if well wrapped.

Yield: 4 dozen

Apricot Covered Cheese Bar

Use our naturally sweetened Apricot Jam or your favorite marmalade or preserves in this easily prepared spread.

Apricot Jam:
½ cup snipped dried apricots
1   cup pineapple juice

¼ cup chopped dates
Also:
1   8-ounce package cream cheese

● Soak apricots in pineapple juice for a few hours or overnight in the refrigerator. ● Purée apricots and juice in a blender with chopped dates. Set cream cheese bar in the center of a 9-inch serving plate. Spoon Apricot Jam over top. ● Serve with crackers or party breads arranged around cream cheese.

Yield: 8 to 12 servings

Guacamole

Our adaptation of Mexico's most popular and versatile avocado dish can be savored as a dip, a salad or a sauce for tacos and tostadas.

1   large ripe avocado
2   tablespoons unflavored yogurt
1   medium-sized scallion, finely chopped
1   small tomato, finely chopped

Dash of hot pepper sauce or more
    to taste
¼   to ½ teaspoon garlic salt
½   to 1 teaspoon lemon juice

● Mash avocado well in a small bowl. Stir in all remaining ingredients, mixing thoroughly. Serve as a dip with taco-flavored corn chips or fresh vegetable sticks.

Variation: Use ½ to 1 tablespoon tamari in place of hot pepper sauce and omit garlic salt.

Yield: about 1 cup

Lentil Pâté

This dish is an adaptation of a traditional Mid-Eastern recipe. It can be served hot or cold, as a pâté with crackers or, in combination with cheese, yogurt dressing and sprouts, tucked into a pita sandwich.

½   cup dried lentils
½   cup uncooked rice
2   cups water
2   tablespoons butter
2   tablespoons vegetable oil

1   large garlic clove, pressed
1   teaspoon ground allspice
1   teaspoon salt
3   medium-sized onions, chopped

● Rinse and drain lentils and rice. Place together in a medium-sized saucepan with 2 cups cold water. Bring to a boil. Reduce heat and simmer covered until water is absorbed and lentils and rice are cooked (about 45 minutes). ● Meanwhile, in a large skillet, gently heat butter, vegetable oil, garlic, allspice and salt. Stir in onions and sauté until soft. ● Combine lentil and onion mixtures. Run the mixture through a food mill or process with the steel blade of a food processor until just puréed. Serve hot or cold on crackers or small rounds of bread.

Note: To serve a molded hors d'oeuvre, pack the pâté into a lightly greased mold or small loaf pan. Chill well. Unmold, place on a serving platter and surround with crisp crackers.

Yield: about 4 cups

New York Dip

Charm your guests with a beautiful basket of freshly prepared crudités alongside a bowl of this zippy dip. Select colorful, crisp vegetables for dipping such as red and green pepper sticks, carrots, radishes, cucumbers, cauliflower or broccoli flowerets and thinly sliced spears of zucchini.

1	8-ounce package cream cheese, at room temperature
1	medium-sized green bell pepper, finely chopped
1	medium-sized onion, finely chopped
½	cup finely chopped sweet gherkins, drained
¼	cup Eggless Mayonnaise

1	teaspoon prepared white horseradish
2	garlic cloves, minced
½	cup chili sauce or Cocktail Sauce
2	cups cottage cheese
	Hot pepper sauce
	Salt and pepper

● Combine all ingredients, adding hot pepper sauce, salt and pepper to taste. Mix thoroughly.

Yield: about 5 cups

Eggplant Caviar

You don't have to be an eggplant lover to enjoy this popular pâté.

1	medium-sized eggplant
1	medium-sized onion, sliced
¼	cup olive oil

¼	cup chopped fresh parsley
1	tablespoon lemon juice
1	teaspoon salt

● Prick eggplant and bake in a pan at 400° F. for 1 hour. ● Allow to cool, then remove skin and cut pulp into small chunks. Squeeze or press excess liquid from eggplant. Sauté onion in 1 tablespoon of the olive oil for about 5 minutes or until transparent. ● Combine remaining olive oil with all ingredients in a blender or food processor and purée. Serve as a dip or spread.

Yield: about 2 cups

Pita Crisps

A tasty, crunchy snack that can be ready in just a few minutes. Can also be used with dips.

2	large pita breads	2	tablespoons grated Parmesan cheese
¼	cup butter		Garlic powder to taste

● Split each pita bread into 2 rounds. Spread inner sides with butter, then sprinkle with Parmesan cheese and garlic powder. Cut each round into 12 wedges. ● Arrange on a baking sheet, cheese side up. Pop under a preheated broiler for a few seconds until the bread is crispy and edges curl.

Yield: 4 dozen

Fresh Vegetable Kabobs

Experiment with this attractive open-ended recipe, selecting a variety of vegetables in season.

Avocado	Artichoke hearts
Green or red bell pepper	Whole or sliced pitted olives
Fresh tomato	Cheese
Fresh or canned mushroom caps	Italian Dressing
Cucumber	

● Cut all vegetables into small, bite-sized chunks or slices for skewering onto long party toothpicks (3 inches or more). Cut cheese into cubes and refrigerate. ● Place vegetables side by side in a shallow dish or on a platter. (Don't mix together or they will be harder to select for skewering.) Drizzle a generous amount of Italian Dressing over top, and turn vegetables to coat. Let marinate at least 1 hour. ● Spear one of each vegetable and cheese on each pick. Use cheese or a firm vegetable such as green pepper at the end of tip to hold vegetables on. If you use the same pattern on each kabob, they will arrange attractively on your serving tray.

Variation: For **Fresh Fruit Kabobs,** skewer chunks or slices of fresh fruit for a naturally sweet and refreshing hors d'oeuvre. Marinate any fruits prone to discoloration (such as apples or pears) in pineapple juice before using.

Note: Plan on 2 kabobs per guest.

Hand-Rolled Sushi

This traditional Japanese dish is an impressive way to start a party. Just set up your sushi bar with its attractive array of ingredients and let your guests do the rest.

1½ ounces unroasted nori sheets
2 cups cooked, short grain brown rice
⅔ cup seasoned rice vinegar
2 medium-sized carrots, peeled and cut into 3-inch, fine julienne strips
1 pound fresh spinach or Oriental mustard greens, trimmed and washed
1 large ripe avocado
1 tablespoon lemon juice
4 ounces firm tofu, cut into julienne strips
½ cup chopped scallions
2 tablespoons vegetable oil

1 3½-ounce bag of enoki mushrooms, brown ends trimmed off
½ cucumber, peeled and cut into 3-inch, fine julienne strips
Pickled sliced ginger
Goma-miso furikake
½ cup tamari
Sesame Sauce:
¾ cup Eggless Mayonnaise
1 tablespoon honey
1 tablespoon toasted sesame seeds
1½ teaspoons Oriental sesame-flavored oil

● Toast each nori sheet by moving back and forth over an electric burner or low gas flame just until nori turns green. *Do not over-toast.* Using scissors, cut into 4- or 5-inch squares. Stack on a plate or place in a serving basket. ● Combine rice and ⅓ cup of the seasoned rice vinegar in a bowl. Mix well and set aside. ● Bring remaining ⅓ cup seasoned rice vinegar to a boil in a small saucepan. Add carrots. Cook and stir until tender-crisp. Drain and set aside. ● Steam spinach or mustard greens until just limp. Drain and set aside. ● Slice avocado into small, thin sections. Moisten all sides with lemon juice to prevent discoloration. Set aside. ● In a small skillet, sauté tofu strips with scallions in vegetable oil until tofu is lightly browned. ● Arrange tofu, carrots, spinach or mustard greens, avocado, mushrooms, cucumber and pickled ginger slices on a tray. Divide the rice between two serving bowls and place alongside tray on your serving table. Add a bowl of goma-miso furikake seasoning and a bowl of tamari. Stir together Sesame Sauce ingredients and serve in two bowls. Place nori sheets on table. ● *To roll sushi,* hold a piece of nori flat in the palm of your hand. Spoon a small amount of seasoned rice into the center. Top with your choice of foods from the sushi tray. (Don't pile too high!) Spoon a little seasoning, Sesame Sauce and/or tamari over filling. Overlap corners to enclose filling.

Note: Check at an Oriental grocery for the specialty items listed. Nori sheets are sometimes available pre-toasted and can be used right from the package.

Yield: 6 servings

Dolmas

One of Greece's outstanding appetizers, Dolmas use marinated grape leaves to house a seasoned rice filling, rich with pine nuts and currants.

3	cups chopped onion	6	tablespoons pine nuts
¾	cup olive oil	½	teaspoon ground cinnamon
1	cup uncooked rice	¼	teaspoon ground allspice
1	teaspoon salt	1	16-ounce jar of grape leaves
	Pinch of black pepper		Boiling water to cover
6	tablespoons currants		Juice of ½ fresh lemon (1½ tablespoons)
1	cup boiling water		

● Sauté onion in ½ cup of the olive oil until soft and transparent. Add rice and stir to coat rice with oil. Mix in salt, pepper and currants. ● Pour in 1 cup boiling water. Stir well and cover tightly. Cook over low heat until liquid is absorbed, about 20 to 30 minutes. Remove from heat and mix in pine nuts, cinnamon and allspice. ● Prepare grape leaves by soaking in hot water for a few minutes. Rinse the leaves and separate them, placing shiny side down on a smooth surface. Use the torn leaves to line the bottom of a Dutch oven (heavy pot with a tight-fitting cover). ● Place a generous teaspoonful of the rice mixture in the center of each leaf. Roll from stem-end upwards, folding in sides to make a tight roll. Lay stuffed grape leaves seam-side down, side by side, on the bed of torn leaves. Drizzle remaining ¼ cup olive oil over top. Add enough boiling water just to cover. Place a heat-proof plate on top of the grape leaf rolls to hold them in place. ● Simmer covered over low heat (250° F.) for 1 hour. Drain, then sprinkle with lemon juice. Let cool before serving.

Yield: 2 dozen

Pakoras

An Indian favorite, these vegetables are dipped in a well-seasoned batter then deep-fried until golden brown and crispy. Choose four or five different vegetables for this popular entrée.

Batter:
2	cups chickpea flour
1	teaspoon salt
¼	teaspoon baking soda
½	teaspoon ground cumin
½	teaspoon pomegranate seeds, crushed (optional)
¼	cup chopped fresh coriander or parsley
1½	cups water

Filling:
Cauliflower flowerets, thinly sliced
Whole mushrooms, trimmed
Sliced eggplant pieces
Broccoli flowerets, thinly sliced
Sliced carrots
Sliced small potatoes, ¼-inch thick
Also:
Vegetable oil for deep-frying

● Prepare batter and your choice of vegetables. Heat oil to a medium-hot temperature (375° F.). For batter, combine first six ingredients. Add water slowly, using up to 1½ cups, until batter is the consistency of pancake batter. When preparing vegetables, cut those which require longer cooking into smaller pieces than the quick-cooking ones. Pat vegetables dry with a paper towel so batter will stick well. ● Dip filling ingredients into batter to coat. Deep-fry 4 to 6 at a time until golden brown. Remove with a slotted spoon and drain on paper towels. ● Serve at once with chutney or ketchup.

Yield: batter for about 2 dozen

Tempura

Tender-crisp vegetables are enveloped in a light, deep-fried batter in this Japanese delicacy.

Batter:
½ cup whole wheat flour
½ cup cornmeal
4 teaspoons cornstarch
1 teaspoon baking powder
½ teaspoon salt
1 cup water
Assorted Vegetables:
   Cauliflower
   Zucchini
   Yams or potatoes
   Eggplant

   Onion
   Broccoli
   Green beans
   Green pepper
   Carrots
   Mushrooms
   Squash blossoms
   Tiger lilies
   Parsley sprigs
Also:
   Peanut or vegetable oil for deep-frying
   Tempura Dipping Sauce (below)

● Prepare batter in advance. Combine all batter ingredients and set aside for ½ hour to thicken. ● *Thinly* slice your choice of vegetables or cut into bite-sized pieces, leaving mushrooms, squash blossoms, tiger lilies and parsley sprigs whole. Pat vegetables dry, then dip into batter and coat well. ● Deep-fry a few at a time in hot oil (375° F.) until coating is golden brown and vegetables inside are cooked but still crisp. Remove from oil with a slotted spoon and drain on paper towels. Serve at once with Tempura Dipping Sauce.

Yield: batter for about 16 pieces

Tempura Dipping Sauce

Serve this sauce with Tempura or other deep-fried Japanese dishes.

2 tablespoons vegetable oil
2 garlic cloves, pressed
¼ cup finely chopped onion
1 teaspoon grated fresh ginger

¼ cup ketchup
1 heaping tablespoon miso, white preferred
¼ teaspoon black pepper
¼ to ½ cup water

● Heat vegetable oil in a small saucepan. Add garlic, onion and ginger. Sauté until onion is soft. ● In a small bowl, stir ketchup, miso and black pepper together until smooth. Add to saucepan. Stir in ¼ to ½ cup water for desired consistency. Bring to a boil, stirring constantly. Remove from heat and serve with Tempura.

Variation: For an Indian touch, add ⅛ teaspoon curry powder and ⅛ teaspoon ground cumin.

Yield: about ¾ cup

Beverages

Banana Smoothie

Try this delicious drink — then use your imagination to concoct your own creations.

2	cups unflavored yogurt	½	cup fresh or frozen strawberries
2	ripe medium-sized bananas	6	ice cubes
½	cup apple or pineapple juice		

● Whirl all ingredients except ice cubes in a blender. Slowly add ice while blending. Process until smooth and thick.

Yield: 4 servings

Hi-Protein Shake

Start your day with a quick, nutritional boost.

⅓	cup raw almonds, cashews or sunflower seeds	1	teaspoon vanilla extract or 1 tablespoon chocolate flavoring
1½	cups milk	1	tablespoon liquid or granular lecithin
1	medium-sized banana	1	tablespoon nutritional yeast (optional)
		1	tablespoon vegetarian protein powder

● Whirl nuts in blender to make a fine textured meal. Add other ingredients and process until puréed.

Note: For a smoother drink, seeds and nuts can be soaked in water overnight before using.

Yield: 2 servings

Watercress Lime Cocktail

An enjoyable combination that is rich in vitamins A and C.

2	cups watercress leaves and small stems	½	cup fresh lime juice
2	cups pineapple juice	2	teaspoons honey
		4	ice cubes

● Process all ingredients except ice cubes in a blender until smooth. Add ice slowly while blending. Serve at once.

Yield: 4 servings

Tangy Tomato Juice

Especially good with guacamole and crispy corn chips.

2   cups chilled tomato juice
2   scallion bulbs with 1-inch of green
    left on
2   tablespoons lemon juice
¼   teaspoon celery seed

1   stalk celery, cut into chunks
    Generous dash of hot pepper sauce
Garnish:
    Cucumber sticks or stalks of leafy celery

● Whirl all ingredients in a blender. Serve in tall glasses garnished with cucumber sticks or celery stalks.

Yield: 2 servings

Cucumber Cooler

Cheese and crackers make a wonderful accompaniment to this rich, satisfying drink.

1   medium-sized cucumber, peeled, cut
    into chunks
2   cups tomato juice
½   ripe medium-sized avocado, cut
    into chunks
1   tablespoon vinegar
1   tablespoon olive oil

⅛   teaspoon salt
    Pinch of fresh basil or
      marjoram (optional)
6   ice cubes
Garnish:
    Lemon wedges

● Purée all ingredients except ice cubes in a blender. Add ice slowly while blender is running. Continue processing until smooth. Serve at once, garnished with a wedge of lemon on rim of glass.

Yield: 4 to 6 servings

Almond Pear Soda

A light, unique blend of flavors.

2   tablespoons lemon juice
2   tablespoons mild-flavored honey
6   tablespoons unflavored yogurt, chilled
½   teaspoon almond extract

⅔   cup pear nectar, chilled
1⅓ cups sparkling water, chilled
Garnish:
    Ground cinnamon or nutmeg (optional)

● Whirl all ingredients except sparkling water in a blender until well mixed. Pour into serving glasses and stir in sparkling water. Garnish with a light sprinkling of cinnamon or nutmeg if desired.

Yield: 2 servings

Icy Grape Frost

A welcome summertime special.

1 cup seedless green grapes	⅔ cup sparkling water, chilled
⅔ cup white grape juice, chilled	

● Wash seedless grapes and freeze until hard. ● Place frozen grapes in a blender with white grape juice. Purée thoroughly for an even, icy texture. Pour into serving glasses and stir in sparkling water.

Yield: 2 servings

Mock Strawberry Daiquiri

A frothy and delightful strawberry drink.

2 cups cold apple juice	1¼ cups frozen, unsweetened strawberries

● Pour apple juice into blender and start processing on low speed. Add strawberries gradually while motor is running. Do not overblend. Serve at once while frothy.

Yield: 3 servings

Citrus Spritzer

Cool, slightly tart and so refreshing.

1 cup orange juice	1½ cups sparkling water
1 cup pineapple juice	Cracked ice
2 tablespoons lemon juice	*Garnish:*
2 tablespoons lime juice	Lemon slices

● Combine fruit juices and sparkling water. Serve over cracked ice, garnished with a lemon slice. Sweeten to taste if desired.

Yield: 4 servings

Beverages

Mock Pineapple Mai Tai

Entertaining? This is ideal for serving with appetizers or hors d'oeuvres.

6   ounces frozen grapefruit juice
        concentrate, undiluted
6   ounces frozen pineapple juice
        concentrate, undiluted
2¼ cups water

1   teaspoon honey
4   ice cubes, cracked
2   tablespoons lime juice
Garnish:
      Lime slices

● Whirl all ingredients together in a blender until frothy. Serve at once in long-stemmed glasses with a garnish of lime slice on the rim of each glass.

Yield: 6 to 8 servings

Fruit Punch

A popular and healthy combination of juices.

1   quart orange juice
1   quart apple juice

2   cups grape juice

● Combine juices and chill. For a simple party punch, serve with Fruit Ice (below).

Yield: 10 servings

Fruit Ice

Use this colorful idea in place of ice cubes for any punch by selecting fruits and juices that complement your beverage.

1   cup water
2   cups orange juice

1   or more cups mixed fresh or canned fruits:
        whole strawberries, sliced peaches,
        apricot halves, seedless grapes,
        pitted cherries, pineapple chunks

● Combine ingredients in a ring or other shaped mold. When filling, leave at least one inch at the top to allow for expansion while freezing. ● Freeze until solid. Just before using, place bottom and sides of mold in warm water to loosen the Fruit Ice. Remove from mold and float Fruit Ice in punch bowl.

Yield: ice for one punch bowl

Festive Sparkling Punch

A delicious and impressive punch for those very special occasions.

3	quarts sparkling apple cider
3	quarts ginger ale
½	gallon orange juice
2	pints sherbet (1 lime and 1 raspberry)

Garnish:
Whole fresh strawberries
Thin orange slices

● Chill all punch ingredients. ● Place sherbet in a large bowl and pour in sparkling cider, ginger ale and orange juice. Stir gently. Garnish with strawberries and/or orange slices.

Yield: 36 servings

Mock Sangria

A good drink served before dinner, with dinner or after dinner.

4	cups grape juice
2	cups orange juice
2	tablespoons lemon juice
4	cups water

Ice
Garnish:
Lemon slices, halved
Orange slices, quartered

● Combine juice and water in a 3-quart pitcher. Pour over ice in long-stemmed glasses. Drop in lemon and orange slices for garnish.

Yield: 12 servings

Creamy Nog

A winter-holiday favorite for children and grown-ups alike.

3	cups milk
1	cup light or heavy cream
¼	cup dry, instant vanilla pudding mix

1   teaspoon vanilla extract or
     ½ teaspoon vanilla and
     ½ teaspoon other extract flavoring
Freshly ground nutmeg

● Combine milk, cream, vanilla pudding mix and extract in a blender. Add a generous pinch of nutmeg. Whirl until well blended. ● Serve chilled. Garnish each serving with a sprinkling of ground nutmeg.

Yield: 6 servings

Beverages

Wassail

Hot, spiced cider is always a seasonal favorite.

1   whole orange
20 whole cloves

1   gallon apple cider or juice
3   cinnamon sticks

● Wash orange. Firmly push cloves into rind. ● Place orange, apple cider or juice and cinnamon sticks in a 6-quart pan. Bring to a boil, then reduce heat to low and simmer covered for 1 hour. Remove the orange if cooking longer to avoid any bitterness. ● Serve hot in mugs. Sweeten if desired.

Note: This can conveniently be made in a large crock pot. Keep on *low* setting for up to several hours.

Yield: 12 to 15 servings

Café Cocoa

Brazilian hot chocolate with a mocha touch.

1   ounce unsweetened baking chocolate
¼   cup sugar
½   cup boiling water
1   cup hot milk

½   cup cream
2   cups fresh hot coffee
1   teaspoon vanilla extract

● Melt chocolate and sugar in a double boiler or over very low heat (chocolate burns easily). Add boiling water and stir until smooth. Heat for 3 to 5 minutes over low heat. ● Stir in hot milk, cream and fresh coffee. Beat or stir briskly until frothy. Add vanilla extract and serve.

Yield: 4 servings

Indian Tea

This flavorful tea is enjoyed throughout the day in India.

2   cardamom pods
3½ cups water
4   teaspoons black tea or 4 tea bags

¾   cup milk
   Sugar to taste

● Break cardamom pods open and drop into water in a 2-quart pan. Bring water to a boil, then add tea and milk. Carefully bring mixture to a second boil. ● Remove from heat. Cover and steep for 5 minutes. Strain and sweeten to taste.

Note: The cardamom seeds can also be removed from the pods and crushed before adding to water for more flavor. In India, tea is traditionally sweetened before serving.

Yield: 4 servings

Soups

Minestrone Soup

Enjoy this festive and distinctive soup as a meal in itself or as a first course to an Italian dinner.

1 large onion, diced
1 cup diced celery
1 garlic clove, minced
3 tablespoons olive oil
1 28-ounce can tomatoes
1 6-ounce can tomato paste
8 cups water
4 vegetable bouillon cubes
8 cups assorted vegetables: chopped carrots, zucchini, cabbage, green beans, fresh spinach, whole peas
1 to 2 teaspoons crumbled dry oregano

1 teaspoon crumbled dry basil
1 tablespoon chopped fresh parsley
1 15-ounce can kidney beans, drained
2 teaspoons salt or to taste
Black pepper to taste
1½ cups uncooked elbow macaroni or broken spaghetti pieces
Italian or French bread, thinly sliced (optional)
Butter and garlic powder (optional)
Grated Parmesan cheese

● Sauté onion, celery and garlic in olive oil in an 8-quart pot until soft. Stir in tomatoes and crush gently. Add tomato paste, water and bouillon cubes. Bring to a boil. ● Add your choice of vegetables, oregano, basil, parsley, kidney beans, salt and pepper. Return to a boil, reduce heat and simmer covered for about 45 minutes. During last 15 minutes of cooking, add macaroni or spaghetti pieces. Add additional water if needed. ● Spread bread slices with butter and sprinkle with garlic powder. Toast on a baking sheet in a 400° F. oven for 5 to 10 minutes until golden. (Watch carefully.) ● Ladle soup into bowls. Place toasted garlic bread on top of soup just before serving. Sprinkle with Parmesan cheese.

Yield: 12 to 16 servings

Pasta Fuccioli

Italy is the home of this legendary pasta and bean soup. Serve with Italian bread and salad for a satisfying soup-supper.

1 6-ounce can tomato paste
4 to 6 cups water
½ cup olive oil
2 garlic cloves, minced
2 tablespoons crumbled dry basil

¼ teaspoon cayenne pepper
Salt to taste
5 cups cooked Great Northern beans
8 ounces uncooked pasta shells or small mostoccoli

● Combine all ingredients except the beans and pasta in a 4-quart pot. Bring to a boil, then reduce heat and simmer covered for 30 minutes. Add beans and simmer an additional 30 minutes. Just before serving, prepare pasta according to package instructions. Drain and add to pot. Serve hot in bowls.

Yield: 6 servings

Split Pea & Rice Soup

We have adapted this national dish of the Netherlands by adding rice, potatoes and carrots, and seasoning it with tamari. The result is a thick, satisfying soup.

6   cups water
3   tablespoons vegetable oil
1   medium-sized onion, chopped
1   teaspoon salt or vegetable salt
1   cup dried split peas

¼   cup uncooked brown rice
2   medium-sized carrots, chopped
1   stalk celery, chopped
1   medium-sized potato, cubed
2   tablespoons tamari or to taste

● Bring water to a full boil in a 4-quart pot. Add all ingredients except tamari. Bring to a second boil. ● Reduce heat and simmer covered for 1¼ to 1½ hours, stirring occasionally. Add more water if soup seems too thick. ● At end of cooking time, stir in tamari. Cover and set aside for at least one hour to thicken. Reheat before serving.

Yield: 6 servings

Smoked Country Soup

Inspired by a Spanish chickpea soup, our version embodies the rich, smoky flavor prized in the Spanish countryside.

6½   cups water
1⅔   cups cooked chickpeas (1 15-ounce can, drained)
5   vegetarian hot dogs, cut into 1-inch pieces
3   cups coarsely chopped cabbage
1   medium-sized carrot, sliced

1   small onion, chopped
1   large potato, cut into ½-inch cubes
1   garlic clove, minced
¼   teaspoon hot pepper sauce
¾   teaspoon salt
⅛   teaspoon black pepper
5   vegetable bouillon cubes

● Start water heating in a 6-quart pan while other ingredients are being prepared. ● Add all remaining ingredients. Bring to a boil, then reduce heat and simmer covered for 30 minutes.

Yield: 8 servings

Chili

Add this winter standby to your list of convenient soups.

3 large onions, chopped	1 cup dry textured soy protein
2 cups sliced celery	1 tablespoon chili powder or to taste
½ cup chopped green bell pepper	½ teaspoon garlic powder
1 16-ounce can tomatoes	1½ teaspoons salt or to taste
1 10¾-ounce can condensed tomato soup	2 tablespoons butter or vegetable oil
2 15-ounce cans kidney beans	2 cups water
	Shredded cheese (optional)

● *For crock pot cooking:* Combine all ingredients except cheese in a 4-quart crock pot. Cook covered on high for 1 hour. Turn heat to low and cook covered for 6 more hours. ● *For conventional cooking:* Combine all ingredients except cheese in a 4- or 5-quart pot. Bring to a boil. Reduce heat and simmer covered for 1 hour. ● Serve with shredded cheese sprinkled on top of chili.

Yield: 6 to 8 servings

Black Bean Soup

Black beans are widely used throughout the Caribbean and Latin America. Try serving this superb soup with our Tofu Tortilla Roll-Ups or Bountiful Burgers.

1 pound dried black beans (2½ cups)	2 tablespoons white vinegar or lemon juice
3 quarts water	Sour cream
2 teaspoons salt or to taste	
2 tablespoons vegetable oil	*Rice Garnish:*
2 tablespoons olive oil	2 cups cooked brown rice
1½ cups chopped onion	¼ to ½ cup finely chopped onion
4 garlic cloves, minced	4 tablespoons olive oil
1 cup chopped green bell pepper	1 to 2 tablespoons white vinegar
2 teaspoons dried parsley	⅔ cup chopped fresh parsley
2 teaspoons crumbled dry oregano	¼ teaspoon salt
1½ teaspoons ground cumin	
¼ teaspoon black pepper	

● Soak beans overnight in 6 to 8 cups water. ● Prepare Rice Garnish in advance by combining all ingredients. Cover and refrigerate to let rice marinate. ● To make soup, discard bean soaking water. Place beans in a 6-quart pot with 3 quarts cold water. Add salt and bring to a boil. Reduce heat and simmer partially covered for 1 to 1½ hours until beans are tender, stirring occasionally. Meanwhile, remove Rice Garnish from refrigerator and let stand to reach room temperature. ● Heat oils in a skillet. Add onion, garlic and green pepper. Sauté until vegetables are tender. Add parsley, oregano, cumin and black pepper. Cook over low heat 3 more minutes. Set aside. ● After beans have cooked, transfer half the beans and liquid to a large container. Add the sautéed vegetables to container. Purée this mixture, 2 cups at a time, in a blender or food processor. Stir back into the soup after puréeing. Add vinegar or lemon juice. Simmer covered for 10 minutes. ● Ladle into bowls. Sprinkle about ¼ cup Rice Garnish over each serving. Add a dollop of sour cream.

Yield: 10 to 12 servings

Soups

Manhattan Vegetable Chowder

Our adaptation of a traditional Manhattan chowder is simple to prepare, fast cooking and satisfying. It's a perfect soup to serve with our Sea Cutlets.

2 tablespoons butter	5 vegetable bouillon cubes
½ cup finely chopped leeks	1½ cups coarsely chopped tomatoes
½ cup chopped onion	1⅔ cups cooked chickpeas (1 15-ounce can)
1 garlic clove, minced	8 ounces firm tofu, crumbled
½ cup chopped green bell pepper	⅓ cup ketchup
½ cup diced carrot	¼ teaspoon crumbled dry thyme
2 cups chopped celery	1 bay leaf, crumbled
3 cups diced potatoes	4 whole cloves, finely crushed
6 cups water	Salt and freshly ground pepper to taste

● Melt butter over low heat in a 6-quart pan. Add leeks, onion and garlic and sauté for 5 minutes. ● Add remaining ingredients. Bring to a boil, reduce heat and simmer covered for 35 more minutes.

Yield: 8 to 10 servings

Mulligatawny Soup

The exciting combination of ingredients used to create this soup reflects a fascinating blend of Indian and English cultures.

3 tablespoons butter	1 green bell pepper, chopped
1 teaspoon curry powder	8 ounces firm tofu, cut into ¾-inch cubes
⅛ teaspoon ground mace or nutmeg	2 medium-sized tomatoes, chopped
⅛ teaspoon ground clove	1 tablespoon chopped fresh parsley
⅛ teaspoon powdered sage	1 cup uncooked brown rice
⅛ teaspoon powdered thyme	6 cups water
1 teaspoon chopped fresh ginger	5 vegetable bouillon cubes
1 medium-sized onion, chopped	1 teaspoon lemon juice
1 medium-sized carrot, thinly sliced	1⅔ cups cooked kidney or pinto beans
or diced	(1 15-ounce can, drained)
1 stalk celery, diced	Black pepper to taste
1 apple, peeled, cored and thinly sliced	1½ teaspoons salt

● Melt butter over low heat in a 6-quart pot. Stir in curry, mace or nutmeg, clove, sage, thyme and ginger. Add onion, carrot, celery, apple, green pepper and tofu. Stir until well mixed. Add remaining ingredients and bring to a boil. ● Reduce heat and simmer covered for 1 hour. Add additional water if soup seems too thick.

Yield: 8 to 10 servings

35

Lentil Soup

Respected for their excellent protein, lentils also provide a base for full-bodied and flavorful soups.

2½ cups dried lentils (1 pound)	2 teaspoons salt
10 cups water	1 teaspoon crumbled dry basil
2 stalks celery cut into 1-inch chunks	1 teaspoon crumbled dry oregano
1 large onion, cut into eighths	3 tablespoons tamari
4 medium-sized carrots, cut into chunks	Black pepper

● Rinse lentils. Add lentils to 7 cups of the water in a 6-quart pot and bring to a boil. ● Whirl celery, onion and carrots with remaining 3 cups water in a blender or food processor until finely chopped. (Blend in batches, using 1 cup of water with each batch.) Add vegetables to lentils. ● Season with salt, basil, and oregano. Return to a boil, reduce heat and simmer covered for 1¼ hours. ● Stir in tamari. Add black pepper to taste.

Yield: 8 to 10 servings

Red Lentil & Vegetable Stew

A time-tested, Mid-Eastern recipe that is quickly prepared. Serve with Hummos in pita bread and Tabbouli Salad for a memorable meal.

8 ounces dried red lentils (1¼ cups)	2 vegetable bouillon cubes
5 cups water	2 garlic cloves, minced
2 medium-sized potatoes, cut into ½-inch chunks	2 tablespoons chopped fresh parsley or 2 teaspoons dried
1 medium-sized onion, chopped	1 teaspoon salt
1 large carrot, halved lengthwise and sliced	1 teaspoon ground cumin
1 cup broccoli or cauliflower flowerets, or string beans, cut into 1-inch pieces	

● Carefully sort and check lentils; rinse. Combine lentils with 5 cups water in a 4-quart pan. Bring to a boil. ● While water is heating, prepare vegetables and add to soup. Stir in bouillon cubes, garlic, parsley, salt and cumin. ● Once soup has boiled, reduce heat and simmer covered for about 20 minutes until potatoes and carrots are cooked.

Yield: 4 to 5 servings

Barley Soup

A steaming bowlful of this wholesome, old-fashioned soup is always welcome.

½ cup uncooked barley, rinsed
2 medium-sized onions, sliced
5 medium-sized carrots, cut into chunks
2 cups chopped celery with leaves
½ cup chopped fresh parsley
6 large fresh mushrooms, sliced
2 tablespoons butter or vegetable oil

¼ teaspoon crumbled dry marjoram
8 vegetable bouillon cubes
1 teaspoon salt
1 pound firm tofu, cubed (optional)
¼ cup uncooked brown rice (optional)
12 cups water

● Combine all ingredients in a 6-quart pot. Bring to a boil then reduce heat to low. Simmer partially covered for 3 or more hours, adding additional water as needed. Long, slow simmering brings out the best flavor in this soup.

Yield: 12 to 16 servings

Navy Bean & Barley Soup

A complete protein soup with a winning taste combination.

2 cups dried navy beans
⅔ cup uncooked barley, rinsed
3 quarts water
1 large onion, chopped
1 garlic clove, minced
1 teaspoon crumbled dry oregano
1 teaspoon crumbled dry basil
    Pinch of crumbled dry marjoram

¼ cup vegetable oil
2 carrots, chopped
2 stalks celery, chopped
½ pound fresh mushrooms, chopped
    (about 2½ cups)
1 tablespoon salt
    Black pepper
5 tablespoons tamari

● Rinse beans. Place beans in a large soup pot with barley and 3 quarts of fresh water. Bring to a boil, then reduce heat and simmer covered for 2 minutes. Remove from heat and let stand covered for 1 hour. ● In a large skillet, sauté onion, garlic, oregano, basil and marjoram in vegetable oil for a few minutes. Stir in carrots, celery and mushrooms. Sauté uncovered for 5 to 10 minutes. ● Stir vegetables into beans and barley. Add salt and black pepper to taste. Bring to a boil; reduce heat and simmer covered over low heat for 1 hour. Stir in tamari. Adjust seasonings before serving.

Yield: 12 to 16 servings

Tamari Vegetable Soup

A medley of garden vegetables in a light tamari broth.

4	cups water	1	medium-sized potato, cubed
¼	cup dried lentils, rinsed	1	medium-sized onion, chopped
¼	cup green peas	2	tablespoons tamari or to taste
¼	cup corn kernels	1	teaspoon crumbled dry basil
¼	cup diced carrots	2	fresh tomatoes, chopped

● Combine all ingredients except tomatoes in a 3- or 4-quart pan. Bring to a boil; reduce heat and simmer covered for 45 minutes. ● Add tomatoes. Cover and simmer another 15 minutes.

Yield: 4 to 6 servings

Cheddar Cheese Soup

Cheddar, England is the home of this mellow and popular soup. For an excellent protein combination, serve with our Soy Burgers or Burritos.

3	tablespoons butter	½	teaspoon paprika
¼	cup grated carrot	2	tablespoons cornstarch or arrowroot
¼	cup minced fresh onion	¼	cup cold milk
¼	cup minced celery	1	cup grated sharp Cheddar cheese
4	cups water		Salt and pepper
3	vegetable bouillon cubes		*Garnish:*
½	teaspoon powdered mustard	2	tablespoons chopped fresh parsley

● Melt butter over low heat in a 2-quart saucepan. Add carrot, onion and celery. Sauté for 5 minutes. Add water, bouillon cubes, mustard and paprika. Simmer covered for 15 minutes. ● Combine cornstarch or arrowroot with milk and stir until smooth. Add to soup, mixing well. Cook uncovered over low heat for 5 minutes. *Do not boil.* Add grated cheese and stir until melted. ● Season to taste with salt and pepper. Serve hot, garnished with fresh parsley.

Yield: 4 servings

Hearty Dry Soup Mix

With this handy mix you can quickly create your own substantial soups at a moment's notice.

1 cup dried split peas	¾ cup uncooked barley
1 cup dried lentils	1 cup uncooked small pasta or
¾ cup uncooked brown rice	broken noodles

● Combine all ingredients and store in a tightly sealed container.

Basic Recipe: ● In a large soup pot combine ¾ cup Hearty Dry Soup Mix (well rinsed), 6 cups water or stock, and 4 to 5 cups assorted chopped or shredded vegetables. (Sauté vegetables in vegetable oil or butter first if desired.) ● Season to taste with tamari, salt, pepper, garlic salt, herbs or your favorite seasonings. Bring to a boil. Reduce heat and simmer covered for about 1½ hours.

Yield: 6 to 8 servings

Hearty Vegetable Soup

This Hearty Vegetable Soup can become a stepping stone to exploring your own creativity in the art of soup making.

1⅓ cups Hearty Dry Soup Mix (above), well rinsed	½ cup chopped fresh parsley
12 cups water	1 tablespoon chopped fresh dill or 1 teaspoon dried
2½ cups cubed butternut squash, peeled and cut into ½-inch chunks	½ cup tiny green peas
1½ cups cubed parsnips or potatoes	1 cup sliced fresh mushrooms
2 medium-sized carrots, sliced	8 vegetable bouillon cubes
1 medium-sized onion, chopped	2 teaspoons salt (see note)
1½ cups chopped string beans	4 tablespoons butter (optional)

● Combine all ingredients in a large soup pot. Bring to a boil. Reduce heat and simmer covered for 1½ hours.

Note: Adjust salt amount depending upon the strength of your bouillon cubes. This soup improves in flavor with time and is even better when served the next day.

Yield: 12 to 16 servings

Chinese Soup

This fragrantly delicious soup, with its wonderful assortment of ingredients, will be an asset to any Chinese meal.

⅓	cup tamari	1	cup chopped broccoli flowerets
¼	teaspoon grated fresh ginger	¼	cup thinly sliced leeks
4	ounces firm tofu, thinly sliced (¼ x ¼ x 1½-inch)	15	Chinese pea pods, fresh or frozen
3	tablespoons light sesame oil	6	water chestnuts, thinly sliced
9	cups water	¾	cup uncooked Chinese noodles, broken into pieces (also called cellophane noodles)
3	vegetable bouillon cubes		Salt
	Freshly ground white pepper		
6	dried black mushrooms		

● Combine tamari and ⅛ teaspoon of the ginger to make a marinade. Marinate tofu slices in this for one hour, turning occasionally. ● Drain tofu, reserving 3 tablespoons marinade for the soup. Saute tofu in sesame oil in a heavy 4-quart pan until browned. Add water, bouillon cubes, remaining ⅛ teaspoon ginger and white pepper to taste. Bring to a boil. Reserve 1 cup broth and simmer remaining broth uncovered for 20 minutes. ● While soup is simmering, soak dried mushrooms in the reserved cup of hot soup broth for 20 minutes. Remove mushrooms from broth, discarding stems. Slice caps and add to soup. Drain broth back into the soup, discarding any sediment. ● Add reserved 3 tablespoons of marinade, broccoli and leeks. Simmer uncovered for 10 minutes. Stir in pea pods, water chestnuts and noodles. Simmer 5 minutes. Add salt to taste.

Yield: 6 to 8 servings

Mock Egg Drop Soup

Start an Oriental meal with this light and quickly prepared soup.

6	vegetable bouillon cubes	½	cup tofu, crumbled and at room temperature
6	cups water		*Garnish:*
2	tablespoons nutritional yeast		Chopped green scallion tops

● Dissolve bouillon cubes in boiling water. Stir in nutritional yeast. ● Pour into six cups. In each cup place 1 tablespoon crumbled tofu. Garnish with scallions. Serve at once.

Yield: 6 servings

Sweet & Sour Cabbage Soup

A country-style Russian soup prepared just the way Grandma used to make it.

2 tablespoons butter or vegetable oil	1 14-ounce can whole peeled tomatoes
1 large onion, chopped	2 teaspoons sour salt (citric acid) if available or ¾ cup lemon juice
3 medium-sized carrots, cut into chunks	1 cup brown sugar (preferred) or ¾ cup mild-flavored honey
1 medium-sized cabbage, coarsely chopped	Salt and pepper
8 cups water	
1 18-ounce can crushed tomatoes	

● Melt butter over low heat in a 6- to 8-quart pot. Sauté onion in butter about 5 minutes or until translucent. Add carrots, cabbage, water and tomatoes. ● Bring to a boil; reduce heat to medium and simmer covered for 45 minutes. ● Add sour salt or lemon juice and brown sugar or honey. Simmer covered for 30 to 60 minutes. Add salt and pepper to taste.

Variation: During last half-hour of cooking, add 1 cup uncooked kasha, 2 cups water and ½ cup raisins for all the taste of stuffed cabbage with none of the work!

Yield: 12 to 14 servings

Curried Cauliflower Soup

The unique flavor of curry mingles with cauliflower for a delightful puréed soup.

1 medium-sized cauliflower, cut into flowerets	2⅓ cups milk
2 tablespoons butter	⅓ cup heavy cream
1 medium-sized onion, sliced	1 teaspoon salt
2 small garlic cloves, minced	Dash of white pepper
1 to 2 teaspoons curry powder	*Garnish:*
½ cup water	⅓ cup unflavored yogurt
	¼ cup sliced almonds, toasted

● Steam flowerets in a small amount of water for about 10 minutes until tender. Drain.
● Meanwhile, melt butter over low heat in a 3- or 4-quart saucepan. Sauté onion in butter several minutes until soft. Add garlic and cook 1 minute. Stir in curry powder and cook 2 minutes. ● Combine onion, cauliflower and ½ cup water in a blender or food processor. Whirl until creamy. Return to saucepan and add milk, cream, salt and pepper. ● Heat slowly *without boiling* before serving. Ladle into soup bowls and garnish with yogurt and sliced almonds.

Note: The strength of curry powder varies. In this recipe we suggest you start with 1 teaspoon curry powder, adding more to taste.

Yield: 6 servings

Corn Chowder

Here we have a fast, easy and popular soup.

1	medium-sized onion, sliced	¾	cup water
1	tablespoon vegetable oil	1	17-ounce can cream-style corn
2	medium-sized potatoes, cooked and diced	1½	cups milk
			Salt and pepper

● Sauté onion in oil until soft and golden. ● Combine all ingredients except salt and pepper in a 2-quart saucepan. Heat thoroughly. Add salt to taste and a generous sprinkling of pepper.

Yield: 4 servings

Potato Leek Soup

Good served all year round — hot or cold, chunky or puréed.

6	medium-sized potatoes, cut into ¾-inch chunks	4	vegetable bouillon cubes
3	large leeks (preferred) or medium-sized onions, thinly sliced	5	cups water
		¼	cup chopped fresh parsley
2	medium-sized carrots, cut into thin 1½-inch strips	6	tablespoons butter
		2	cups milk
1	cup chopped celery with leaves		Salt and pepper

● Combine all ingredients except milk, salt and pepper in a 6-quart pan or crock pot. Bring to a boil; reduce heat to medium and cook covered for 25 minutes or until potatoes are tender. (If using a crock pot, cook on high for 3 to 4 hours.) ● Add milk. Season with salt and pepper to taste. Heat before serving *without boiling*.

Note: For a soup with a velvety texture, purée in a blender or food processor after cooking. Serve hot or cold.

Yield: 8 servings

Mock Chicken Noodle Soup

Lots of noodles in a clear broth that relies on fresh dill for its aromatic flavor. A good first course soup.

5 ounces fresh dill (1½ bunches)
2 ounces fresh parsley (1 bunch)
1 medium-sized onion, scored
2 medium-sized carrots, halved lengthwise, cut into 2-inch chunks
2 medium-sized parsnips, halved lengthwise, cut into 2-inch chunks
2 large stalks celery, halved

1 medium-sized turnip, halved and quartered
2 teaspoons salt
1 tablespoon vegetable broth powder or 3 vegetable bouillon cubes
10 cups water
2 ounces capellini (small, thin Italian noodles), broken into thirds

● Tie a string around dill and parsley stalks for easy removal later. Combine all ingredients except noodles in a 6-quart pan. Bring to a boil; reduce heat and simmer covered for 1½ hours. ● Remove dill and parsley. Simmer 10 minutes uncovered. For best flavor, cover soup and refrigerate several hours or overnight. ● Remove vegetables. Boil noodles in soup broth for 6 minutes. Slice carrots and parsnips and return to soup if desired.

Yield: 8 to 10 servings

French Onion Soup Au Gratin

Masters in the culinary arts, the French created this inimitable soup which is savored throughout the world.

3 large onions, sliced
3 tablespoons butter or vegetable oil
5 cups water
5 vegetable bouillon cubes
1 bay leaf
1 tablespoon tamari

Salt and pepper
6 slices French bread, toasted
6 ounces Swiss cheese, sliced or shredded
Grated Parmesan cheese

● Using a 3- or 4-quart saucepan, sauté onions in butter or oil over medium-low heat for about 35 minutes until onions are golden but not browned. Stir frequently. ● Add water, bouillon cubes and bay leaf, and bring to a boil. Reduce heat and simmer covered for 30 minutes. Remove bay leaf. Add tamari and mix well. Adjust seasoning with salt and pepper. ● Ladle into six individual oven-proof serving bowls. Float a slice of toasted French bread in each bowl. Top with Swiss cheese. Sprinkle with Parmesan cheese. Place in a 400° F. oven for about 5 minutes or until cheese is melted and golden.

Yield: 6 servings

Light Mushroom Soup

This soup's flavor captures the essence of mushrooms in a delightful broth.

4   tablespoons butter
1   pound fresh mushrooms, sliced
      (about 5 cups)
4   tablespoons unbleached white flour
6   cups hot water

5   vegetable bouillon cubes
½   cup heavy cream
1   tablespoon lemon juice
Garnish:
     Chopped fresh parsley

● Melt butter over low heat in a 4-quart pan. Add mushrooms and sauté for 3 minutes. Sprinkle flour in, a little at a time, stirring constantly. Add hot water gradually, stirring constantly to avoid lumps. Drop in bouillon cubes and simmer uncovered for 10 minutes. Stir occasionally. ● Remove from heat. Add heavy cream and lemon juice. If desired, purée all or half of the soup in a blender or food processor. ● Just before serving, heat soup *without boiling.* Ladle into bowls. Garnish with fresh parsley.

Yield: 6 servings

Tahini Squash Soup

An interesting puréed soup that has a wonderful creamy texture without the use of any dairy products. An ideal soup to serve with one of our bean and grain burgers.

2   cups diced onion
2   teaspoons vegetable oil
1   medium-sized butternut squash
5   cups water or vegetable stock
¼   cup tahini

1   tablespoon tamari
     Salt
Garnish:
     Chopped fresh parsley
     Toasted sesame seeds

● Sauté onion in vegetable oil in a 4-quart pot until translucent. ● Meanwhile, peel squash and cut into 1-inch cubes. Add to the onion and cover with 5 cups water or vegetable stock. Bring to a boil, then reduce heat and simmer covered for about 30 minutes or until squash is soft. ● Let soup cool slightly for easy handling. Purée in batches in a blender or food processor, adding tahini during the last batch. Return to soup pot after puréeing. ● Season with tamari and salt to taste. Simmer 10 minutes. ● Garnish with chopped parsley and/or toasted sesame seeds.

Yield: 6 servings

Soups

Gazpacho

Spain has provided us with this most refreshing, uncooked soup. A hostess' delight, it is made in advance and served chilled.

1 cucumber, finely chopped, peeled if desired	¼ cup lemon juice
1 onion, finely chopped	2 tablespoons tamari
1 green bell pepper, coarsely chopped	2 tablespoons chopped fresh parsley or 2 teaspoons dried
2 ripe tomatoes, coarsely chopped, peeled if desired	1 large garlic clove, pressed
4 cups tomato juice	Dash of hot pepper sauce or to taste
¼ cup olive oil	*Garnish:*
¼ cup apple cider vinegar	Lemon slices

● Combine ingredients and chill in refrigerator for several hours. For a classic touch, purée half the mixture in a blender or food processor, then return it to the rest of the soup. ● Serve cold, garnished with a half slice of lemon on rim of bowl.

Yield: 6 servings

Fruit Soup

Originating in Poland and Russia, this recipe makes marvelous use of summer fruits and berries. Enjoy it as an elegant luncheon soup, or add a scoop of ice cream for a special dessert.

7 medium-sized or large ripe peaches, cut into quarters	1 pint fresh blueberries
12 Italian purple plums or 7 regular plums, halved	2 cups water
	Mild-flavored honey
2 cups seedless green grapes	Sugar

● In a 6-quart pan, layer pitted peaches and plums, followed by grapes and then blueberries. Add 2 cups water and bring to a boil. Reduce heat and simmer covered for 20 minutes. Stir blueberries down occasionally to be sure they cook. ● When peaches are tender, sweeten soup to taste with honey and sugar. The amount will depend on the natural sweetness of the fruit. Start with 2 tablespoons honey, then 2 tablespoons sugar, adding more until desired sweetness is reached. ● Cover pot and set aside to cool. Purée in blender or food processor if desired. Serve chilled, with sweet cream, sour cream or yogurt.

Yield: 8 to 10 servings.

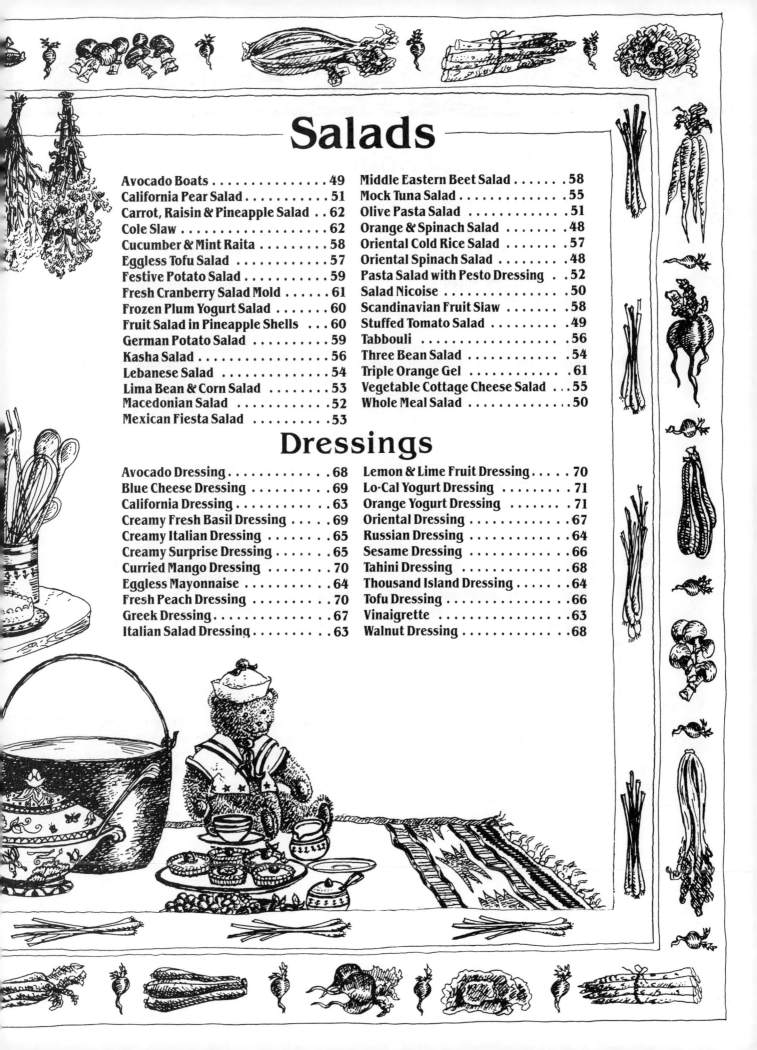

Salads

Dressings

Oriental Spinach Salad

Try this Oriental creation that tastes as sublime as it looks.

½	pound fresh spinach (4 cups torn)	6	cherry tomatoes, halved
1	cup fresh bean sprouts	8	fresh Chinese pea pods (optional)
4	large fresh mushrooms, sliced	4	teaspoons sesame seeds
4	water chestnuts, sliced		Oriental Salad Dressing

● Cover four salad plates with 1 cup spinach each. Place ¼ cup bean sprouts in center of each. Arrange mushrooms, water chestnuts, tomatoes and pea pods around sprouts. ● Toast sesame seeds in an ungreased skillet over medium heat until they start to pop. Remove from heat. Serve with Oriental Salad Dressing and sesame seeds for sprinkling on top.

Yield: 4 servings

Orange & Spinach Salad

This distinctive salad offers an inspired combination of textures and flavors.

1	large avocado, cubed	8	slices fresh orange, peeled and quartered
1	cup Italian Dressing	½	cup thinly sliced Swiss cheese
½	pound thinly sliced fresh mushrooms	***Walnut Croutons:***	
4	slices red onion, separated into rings	1	tablespoon butter
5	cups torn spinach, well rinsed	¼	teaspoon salt
	(1 large bunch)	½	cup walnut pieces

● Measure out ¼ cup of avocado cubes and set remainder aside. Purée the ¼ cup avocado with 1 cup Italian Dressing in a blender. ● Combine mushrooms, remaining avocado cubes and onion rings in a shallow dish. Pour dressing over top and chill for one hour. ● Prepare Walnut Croutons: Melt butter over low heat. Add salt and walnut pieces. Stir and cook over medium heat until nuts are lightly toasted. Set aside to cool. ● Pat spinach leaves dry. Place on a serving platter. Drain the chilled vegetables, saving dressing. Spoon vegetables over spinach. Arrange orange slices and Swiss cheese over top. ● Serve with remaining dressing and garnish with Walnut Croutons.

Yield: 4 servings

Salads

Avocado Boats

A creative way to serve avocado. Nature has graciously provided a natural cavity to house a variety of tempting fillings.

1 medium-sized avocado	2 small scallions
Lemon juice	Paprika
Lettuce leaves	½ cup sprouts
½ cup Tabbouli	Black olives

● Slice avocado in half lengthwise and remove pit. Peel if desired. Sprinkle with lemon juice. Place on a bed of lettuce on individual serving plates. ● Fill center with Tabbouli. Partially insert white end of scallion into narrow end of avocado to form a "mast." Sprinkle filling with paprika. Surround avocado with sprouts and olives.

Variations: Fill avocado with Mock Tuna Salad, Hummos or Eggless Tofu Salad. For **Avocado Cheese Boats,** fill center of avocado with warm chili or other seasoned beans. Top with shredded cheese and place under the broiler until cheese is melted and lightly browned. Serve as above.

Yield: 2 servings

Stuffed Tomato Salad

Make this lovely salad when you have flavorful, ripe and firm tomatoes. Depending on your choice of fillings, stuffed tomatoes can be served as a side dish or a complete luncheon or supper salad.

4 medium-sized tomatoes	1 small cucumber, sliced
Torn lettuce leaves	4 large fresh mushrooms, sliced
1 cup alfalfa sprouts or other filling	California Dressing
(see variations)	

● Remove stems from tomatoes. Partially cut each tomato into 6 or 8 wedges, almost through to the bottom. ● Place tomato on a bed of lettuce on individual salad plates. Gently spread wedges apart. Pile ¼ cup sprouts in center of each tomato. Arrange cucumber and mushroom slices alternately around tomato. ● Serve with California Dressing.

Variations: Use 1 cup Eggless Tofu Salad, Mock Tuna Salad, Tabbouli Salad, or Vegetable Cottage Cheese Salad from this chapter. When using these flavorful fillings, the salad can be served without dressing, or you can select any compatible dressing.

Yield: 4 servings

Whole Meal Salad

An extravaganza of highly nutritious ingredients.

4 cups mixed dark greens	1 tablespoon toasted sesame seeds
1 cup thinly sliced celery	2 tablespoons sunflower seeds
1 cup shredded red cabbage	2 tablespoons slivered almonds
1 cup halved and thinly sliced cucumber	4 radishes, sliced
¼ pound thinly sliced fresh mushrooms (about 1¼ cups)	1 cup cottage cheese
1 large tomato, diced	1 cup shredded zucchini
1 cup cooked pinto beans	1 cup shredded carrot
½ cup coarsely chopped fresh parsley	1 cup alfalfa sprouts
3 tablespoons grated Parmesan cheese	1 cup dressing

● Toss all ingredients together except last five and divide between four serving plates. ● Top each with ¼ cup cottage cheese. Surround with zucchini, carrot and sprouts. Serve with your favorite dressing.

Yield: 4 entrée salads

Salad Nicoise

This artistically combined specialty is a favorite on the Riviera. Serve with a loaf of crusty French bread.

1 medium-sized head Boston lettuce	2 small tomatoes, cut into wedges
4 new potatoes, boiled or steamed	10 slices mozzarella cheese (2 x 1 x ½-inch)
1 cup Vinaigrette	10 pitted black olives
½ pound whole string beans, cooked and drained	10 slices red bell pepper, cut top to bottom, ½-inch wide
1½ cups Mock Tuna Salad	

● Wash and drain lettuce. Place in a plastic bag and refrigerate to crisp. ● Peel potatoes and slice to ⅜-inch thickness. Place in a wide bowl. Pour about ⅓ of the Vinaigrette dressing over potatoes. Toss gently to coat. Cover and set aside. ● Place string beans in a small bowl and pour ⅓ of the Vinaigrette over them. Toss to coat and cover. Let string beans and potatoes marinate for 1 hour, stirring occasionally. ● To arrange salad, place lettuce leaves over the surface of a 14-inch platter or pizza pan. Mound Mock Tuna Salad in the center. Remove potato slices from dressing and lay slices flat around the outside of platter to form a rim. Arrange string beans, tomatoes, cheese, olives and red bell pepper slices around Mock Tuna Salad in an attractive design. ● Serve with remaining dressing.

Yield: 5 servings

California Pear Salad

You will find a fascinating array of flavors in this attractive California salad.

1	15-ounce can kidney beans
1	15-ounce can chickpeas
4	large ripe Bartlett pears, cored and halved
1¾	cups torn lettuce leaves
	Small whole lettuce leaves, Bibb or Boston
12	cherry tomatoes, halved
12	slices sweet pickle

1	medium-sized onion, sliced
6	slices Swiss cheese, about 4 x 4-inches, at room temperature
6	slices caraway cheese, about 4 x 4-inches, at room temperature
6	slices provolone cheese, about 4 x 4-inches, at room temperature
	California Dressing

● Rinse and drain kidney beans and chickpeas. Set aside. ● Cut two of the pear halves into small slices and toss with torn lettuce leaves in a large salad bowl or use a platter. Make a rim of lettuce leaves around edge of bowl or platter, tucking small lettuce leaves in. ● Pile kidney beans and chickpeas side by side in center of lettuce. Arrange tomatoes, pickles and onions around them. ● Using one of each kind of cheese, layer one on top of the other and roll up. Spear with toothpick if desired. Repeat, making five more rolls. Arrange on one side of bowl. On opposite side, place pears on end, side by side. ● Serve at once with California Dressing.

Yield: 6 entrée salads

Olive Pasta Salad

An ideal salad for potlucks or picnics.

1	pound uncooked elbow macaroni or small pasta
4	medium-sized tomatoes, cut into wedges or 18 cherry tomatoes, halved
1	cup pitted black olives or ½ cup black and ½ cup green olives

1	6-ounce jar marinated artichoke hearts with marinade (optional)
⅔	cup cubed Swiss cheese or smoked mozzarella
1	cup Italian Dressing

● Cook pasta in boiling water according to package instructions. Drain in a colander, then rinse under cold running water until cooled. ● Combine pasta with tomatoes, olives, artichokes and cheese. Pour Italian Dressing over salad and toss well. ● Refrigerate until well chilled. Serve cold.

Yield: 6 servings

Pasta Salad with Pesto Dressing

A chilled pasta salad is always a treat, especially when tossed in this piquant basil dressing.

Dressing:
1 cup fresh parsley
½ cup pine nuts or raw cashews
2 garlic cloves, pressed
¼ cup chopped fresh basil or more
  to taste
½ cup grated Parmesan cheese
¼ cup water
1 cup Eggless Mayonnaise

1 tablespoon fresh lemon juice
Salt and pepper to taste
Salad:
1 pound elbow macaroni, cooked, rinsed
  and drained
½ cup sliced scallions
1½ cups fresh or frozen (thawed) green peas
1 cup pitted black olives

● Combine first 6 ingredients for dressing in a blender or food processor and whirl until puréed. Add Eggless Mayonnaise and lemon juice. Process until well blended. Season with salt and pepper. ● Combine salad ingredients in a large bowl. Pour pesto dressing over the salad and toss well. Serve at room temperature.

Note: Fresh basil is always preferred in pesto recipes, but if not available, substitute 2 tablespoons crumbled dry basil. For best flavor, sauté dried basil briefly in a small amount of olive oil or butter before using.

Yield: 8 servings

Macedonian Salad

Whole mushrooms, olives, cherry tomatoes and chickpeas abound in this authentic recipe from the Mediterranean.

1 cup pitted black olives
½ cup pitted green olives
20 cherry tomatoes
1 green bell pepper, diced
1 large onion, chopped or 1 bunch
  scallions, chopped
2 cups cooked chickpeas

20 small fresh mushroom caps
Dressing:
1 cup unflavored yogurt
1 tablespoon lemon juice
2 tablespoons olive oil
½ teaspoon salt

● Combine all salad ingredients. ● Stir together dressing ingredients. Toss salad with dressing just before serving, or serve dressing at the table.

Yield: 6 to 8 servings

Lima Bean & Corn Salad

The flavors of corn, lima beans and cheese complement each other in this easily prepared salad.

1 cup frozen corn kernels	1½ teaspoons prepared mustard
1 cup frozen baby lima beans	Crisp salad greens
½ cup shredded Cheddar cheese	*Garnish:*
2 tablespoons chopped onion	Chopped fresh parsley
3 tablespoons Eggless Mayonnaise	Paprika

● Set frozen corn kernels aside to defrost. Simmer lima beans in ½-inch of water for 10 to 15 minutes until just tender. Drain and cool. ● When limas have cooled, add defrosted corn, cheese, onion, Eggless Mayonnaise and mustard. Toss well. ● Serve on a bed of salad greens. Garnish with fresh parsley and/or paprika.

Yield: 4 servings

Mexican Fiesta Salad

You will enjoy this satisfying salad topped with our Avocado Dressing and garnished with shredded Cheddar cheese and crunchy corn chips.

4 cups torn lettuce leaves	4 slices red onion, separated into rings
1⅔ cups cooked pinto or kidney beans (1 15-ounce can, drained)	8 slices red or green bell pepper
16 pitted black olives	½ cup shredded Cheddar cheese
16 cucumber slices	Corn chips, crumbled
4 small tomatoes, quartered	Avocado Dressing
	Crushed dry red peppers (optional)

● Line a serving bowl or platter with lettuce leaves. Pile beans in the center. Arrange olives, cucumber, tomatoes, onion and bell pepper around beans in an attractive pattern. ● Place cheese, crumbled corn chips and dressing in three separate serving bowls. Let each person garnish their own salad with cheese, chips and dressing. For extra spice, crushed red peppers can be sprinkled on top.

Yield: 4 servings

Lebanese Salad

The Lebanese have a wonderful talent for combining nutritious ingredients that also satisfy the palate. This salad is a good source of iron.

1 cup (packed) chopped fresh parsley
4 scallions, finely sliced
12 cherry tomatoes, quartered or 3 small
    tomatoes, chopped
¾ cup toasted wheat germ
½ cup cooked chickpeas (optional)

Dressing:
3 tablespoons lemon juice
2 tablespoons olive oil
2 tablespoons peanut or soy oil
1 tablespoon tamari

● Combine all salad ingredients in a salad bowl. ● Mix together dressing ingredients. Pour over salad. Toss and serve.

Yield: 2 generous servings

Three Bean Salad

A substantial and colorful bean salad.

1 cup cooked chickpeas
¾ cup cooked kidney beans
¾ cup cooked pinto or cannelli beans
3 tablespoons chopped red onion
⅓ cup shredded carrots
½ cup cooked or uncooked string beans,
    cut into ½-inch pieces (optional)

2 scallions, finely sliced
1 tablespoon chopped fresh chives
1 tablespoon finely chopped fresh dill or
    ½ teaspoon dried
½ teaspoon crumbled dry basil
    Salt and pepper to taste
¼ to ½ cup Vinaigrette

● Combine salad ingredients in a medium-sized bowl. Pour dressing over salad. Toss well.
● Refrigerate for several hours for best flavor.

Yield: 4 servings

Mock Tuna Salad

Undoubtedly one of our outstanding salads. Perfect as a salad, in a sandwich, or as an appetizer with crackers.

1½ cups dry textured soy protein (T.V.P.)	1 pound firm tofu, drained
⅔ cup warm water	1½ cups Eggless Mayonnaise
2 carrots, grated	1½ tablespoons tamari
3 stalks celery, finely chopped	1 tablespoon prepared mustard
2 tablespoons finely chopped fresh parsley (optional)	1 teaspoon lemon juice
2 tablespoons finely chopped scallion (optional)	Salt and pepper to taste

● Combine T.V.P. and warm water in a bowl. Add carrots, celery, parsley and scallion. Mix well. Crumble in tofu. ● Mix together the Eggless Mayonnaise, tamari, mustard, lemon juice and salt and pepper. Add to bowl. Mix thoroughly. ● Refrigerate at least 1 hour.

Note: T.V.P. is available at health food stores.

Yield: 12 servings

Vegetable Cottage Cheese Salad

Our medley of finely chopped vegetables mixed with cottage cheese makes a wonderful low-calorie salad.

½ cup chopped red bell pepper	⅓ cup (scant) sunflower seeds
½ cup chopped cucumber	¾ cup cottage cheese
½ cup chopped fresh parsley	1 tablespoon tamari
½ cup chopped fresh tomato	2 tablespoons grated Parmesan cheese (optional)
2 large scallions, finely sliced	Lettuce leaves
½ cup alfalfa sprouts	

● Toss all ingredients (except lettuce) together until well mixed. Serve on a platter of lettuce leaves.

Note: If not serving immediately, reserve alfalfa sprouts, adding them just before serving.

Yield: 2 cups

Tabbouli Salad

Unquestionably the most popular salad the Lebanese have shared with the West.

1½ cups uncooked fine bulgur
1½ cups boiling water
2 cups chopped fresh parsley
1 bunch scallions, finely chopped
1 large tomato, chopped
3 tablespoons olive oil
3 tablespoons lemon juice

1 tablespoon crumbled dry mint or
   6 tablespoons chopped fresh
1 teaspoon salt
1 garlic clove, minced or ¼ teaspoon
   powder (optional)
Freshly ground black pepper to taste

● Pour boiling water over bulgur in a large bowl. Let stand 1 hour. Return bulgur to bowl.
● Add all other ingredients. Toss well. ● Cover and chill at least 2 hours before serving.

Yield: 6 to 8 servings

Kasha Salad

Kasha (roasted buckwheat kernels) is an exceptionally nutritious grain widely used in Russia. We have combined it with assorted vegetables in this delicious, cold marinated salad.

1 tablespoon vegetable oil
1 cup uncooked kasha, medium grain
1 teaspoon salt
⅛ teaspoon black pepper
2 cups boiling water
2 medium-sized carrots, shredded
1½ scallions, finely sliced

½ cup diced celery
½ cup frozen peas, thawed
¼ to ½ cup chopped fresh parsley
⅔ cup cooked chickpeas
1 teaspoon chopped fresh dill
1 cup Vinaigrette

● Heat oil in a 2-quart saucepan. Add kasha, salt and pepper. Stir constantly over medium heat for about 2 minutes. ● Add boiling water. Cover and reduce heat to low. Cook for 10 to 15 minutes or until kasha is tender. Set aside (covered) to cool. ● When cooled, stir in vegetables and chickpeas. Pour Vinaigrette over kasha. Toss and serve at room temperature.

Yield: 6 servings

Oriental Cold Rice Salad

A cold grain salad with a unique mixture of flavors.

⅔ cup green peas, fresh or frozen	10 water chestnuts, finely sliced
10 Chinese pea pods, fresh or frozen	2 tablespoons chopped fresh chives or
2 teaspoons peanut oil	1½ teaspoons dried
2 cups cooked brown rice	¼ cup Oriental Dressing
1 cup mung bean sprouts	

● Steam fresh peas for 3 minutes, or defrost frozen peas. ● Rinse fresh Chinese pea pods in cold water. Remove stems and strings along top and bottom, leaving pods whole. Stir-fry pea pods in peanut oil for a few minutes until tender-crisp. If using frozen pea pods, defrost and stir-fry just to quickly heat through. Set steamed green peas and Chinese pea pods aside to cool. ● Combine rice, bean sprouts, chestnuts and chives in a bowl. Add cooled peas and pea pods. Pour Oriental Dressing over all. Toss well. Chill for several hours before serving.

Yield: 6 servings

Eggless Tofu Salad

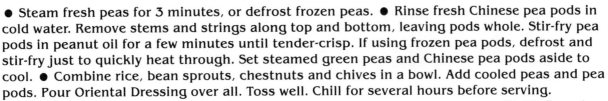

A very popular salad that also doubles as a great sandwich spread.

1 pound firm tofu, crumbled and well-drained	½ teaspoon tamari
	¼ teaspoon garlic powder
2 small stalks celery, minced	1 teaspoon ground turmeric
1 medium-sized carrot, grated	⅛ teaspoon paprika
½ cup Eggless Mayonnaise	¼ teaspoon celery seed
1 tablespoon prepared mustard	⅛ teaspoon black pepper
1 teaspoon salt	Dash of cayenne pepper (optional)

● Mash tofu in a large mixing bowl. Add celery and carrot and mix well. In a separate bowl, combine remaining ingredients. Add to tofu and vegetables, blending well. Chill before serving.

Yield: 3½ to 4 cups

Scandinavian Fruit Slaw

A memorable combination of fruits, cabbage, cheese and nuts in a wonderful yogurt dressing.

2 large oranges, peeled and cut into bite-sized sections	1 cup shredded Cheddar or jack cheese
2 large apples, chopped (peel if desired)	**Dressing:**
1 cup seedless green or red grapes, halved	½ cup Eggless Mayonnaise
¼ cup currants	½ cup unflavored yogurt
1 cup chopped walnuts	2 tablespoons orange juice
2½ cups shredded cabbage	1 tablespoon lemon juice
	1 tablespoon honey or to taste

● Toss salad ingredients in a large bowl. ● Combine dressing ingredients. Mix well. Gently stir dressing into salad. Serve chilled or at room temperature. Use within 2 days.

Yield: 6 servings

Middle Eastern Beet Salad

A very easy, very different chilled beet salad.

6 medium-sized or 4 large beets, cooked and cooled	1 teaspoon whole cumin seed
	Salt and pepper to taste
3 tablespoons fresh lemon juice	Lettuce leaves

● Peel and slice beets. Mix together lemon juice, cumin seed, salt and pepper. Toss with beets. ● Serve cold on a bed of lettuce leaves.

Yield: 6 servings

Cucumber & Mint Raita

A cool, refreshing yogurt salad from India. Usually served to balance the spicy main dishes served in Indian meals.

2 cups unflavored yogurt	½ teaspoon salt or to taste
2 tablespoons minced fresh mint or 2 teaspoons dried	¾ teaspoon ground cumin
1 cucumber, peeled and diced	Freshly ground black pepper

● Stir yogurt briskly in a bowl until smooth. Add mint, cucumber, salt and cumin. ● Place in a serving dish. Grind black pepper over top. Serve cold in small bowls as a side dish.

Yield: 4 servings

Festive Potato Salad

Here is an exciting change from the usual potato salad.

1   6-ounce can pitted small black
      olives, drained
6   cups diced cooked potato, cooled
½   cup chopped raw celery
½   cup chopped raw carrot
½   cup cooked corn kernels
½   cup chopped fresh parsley
¼   cup chopped red onion

1   cup Eggless Mayonnaise
½   teaspoon dried dill weed
¼   teaspoon freshly ground black pepper
1   teaspoon salt (optional)
      Lettuce leaves
Garnish:
      Parsley sprigs

● Reserve 8 olives for topping. Mix remaining olives with potatoes, celery, carrot, corn, parsley and red onion. ● Stir together Eggless Mayonnaise, dill weed, black pepper and salt. Add to potato and vegetables. Toss gently until well mixed. ● Line a platter or bowl with lettuce leaves. Pile salad over lettuce, leaving a border of lettuce. Garnish with reserved olives and parsley sprigs.

Yield: 8 servings

German Potato Salad

Germany has shared many potato recipes with the world, and this is one of the most well-known.

5   large potatoes, unpeeled
1   medium onion, finely chopped
1   teaspoon sugar
¼   cup vinegar
½   cup vegetable broth
1   tablespoon vegetable oil

½   teaspoon salt
      Dash of black pepper
½   cup chopped sweet pickles
2   tablespoons dairy sour cream
1   teaspoon prepared mustard

● Boil potatoes in water until tender. Cool completely. ● Remove potato skins. Cut potatoes in half lengthwise, then into ¼-inch slices. ● Mix remaining ingredients together in a large bowl. Add potatoes and toss gently. Serve cold or warm.

Yield: 4 servings

Frozen Plum Yogurt Salad

A refreshing change-of-pace meal on a hot summer day.

2½ cups sliced fresh plums (about 1¼ pounds)	½ cup chopped pecans or walnuts
2 tablespoons honey or more to taste	1 banana, sliced
1 tablespoon sugar	Lettuce leaves
1 cup unflavored yogurt	Assorted fresh fruits: sliced peaches, strawberries, grapes, blueberries
¼ cup fresh blueberries	Fresh Peach Sauce (optional)

● Bring plums, honey and sugar to a boil in a saucepan. Reduce heat and simmer 5 minutes until soft. Remove from heat. Stir in yogurt and blueberries. Add more sweetener if desired, depending on tartness of plums. Let cool. ● Add chopped nuts and banana, stirring gently. Spoon into paper-lined muffin tins. Place muffin tins in a plastic bag and seal, or cover with foil. Freeze until firm. ● Remove from freezer 15 minutes before serving. To serve, arrange lettuce leaves on serving plates. Place a Frozen Plum Yogurt Salad in center (in paper liner). Surround with assorted fresh fruits. Serve as is, or with Fresh Peach Sauce.

Yield: 12 salads

Fruit Salad in Pineapple Shells

These beautiful, filled pineapple shells are perfect for parties or buffet tables.

1 fresh medium-sized pineapple	½ cup raisins
1 banana, sliced	1 cup cheese cubes (optional)
2 small apples, cut into bite-sized pieces	1½ cups Lemon & Lime Fruit Dressing
2 pears, cut into bite-sized pieces	¼ cup shredded coconut
1 cup seeded grapes	
1 11-ounce can mandarin oranges, drained	

● Rinse whole pineapple, then pat dry with a towel. Halve pineapple lengthwise, cutting through leafy stem (leave stem on). Cut out fruit of pineapple, leaving shell intact. Discard core. Cut pineapple fruit into bite-sized chunks. ● Combine all ingredients except coconut in a bowl. Toss well. Generously fill both pineapple shells with fruit. Sprinkle with shredded coconut. Keep remaining fruit in refrigerator for refilling shells.

Yield: 6 to 8 servings

Triple Orange Gel

Try this orange gel salad and get acquainted with the usefulness of agar.

2   cups fresh orange juice
2   teaspoons agar flakes (not granules)
1½ tablespoons sugar (optional)

2   oranges, peeled, sectioned and cut
     into pieces
     Orange flavored yogurt

● Pour juice into a 1-quart saucepan. Sprinkle in agar flakes. *Bring to a full rolling boil,* stirring constantly. Reduce heat and simmer uncovered for 5 minutes. Stir in sugar and set aside to cool for about ½ hour. ● Place orange pieces in a shallow dish. Pour agar mixture over them. Refrigerate until set, then cut into squares. ● Serve chilled, with a spoonful of orange flavored yogurt on top.

Yield: 6 servings

Fresh Cranberry Salad Mold

Chock-full of fruits, nuts and cranberries, this molded salad will brighten your holiday table.

1   large navel orange, unpeeled
¾ cup orange juice
3   tablespoons agar flakes (not granules)
1   pound fresh cranberries (about 4 cups)
2   large firm apples, cored, unpeeled
2   cups walnuts

1   cup coconut flakes
1   cup sugar or mild-flavored honey
Garnish:
     Lettuce leaves
     Fresh parsley
     Orange slices

● Squeeze juice from orange, saving rind. Pour into a small saucepan. Add ¾ cup orange juice. Sprinkle agar flakes into juice. Let stand 5 minutes to soften. Bring to a boil, then reduce heat and simmer about 10 minutes. Set aside. ● Reserve about 12 cranberries for use as garnish. Process remaining cranberries, orange rind (cut into chunks), apples, and walnuts in a food processor using the metal blade, or in a blender until coarsely chopped. (Process in batches.) Combine in a large bowl with coconut flakes and sugar or honey. Mix well. Stir in agar mixture, scraping saucepan well. ● Pack mixture into a 6- to 8-cup ring or decorative mold. Chill at least 1 to 2 hours until set. ● Unmold by briefly placing bottom of mold in a pan of warm water until edges loosen. Reverse mold onto a serving plate. Arrange lettuce around edges. Garnish with flat parsley leaves and reserved fresh cranberries, halved. Cranberry halves and parsley can be arranged to look like holly for holiday season. Place orange slices on top or around edge of mold. Serve as a salad or a relish.

Note: Color is best when served soon after salad has set. If made with honey, a small amount of liquid may separate and need to be drained off before serving.

Yield: 8 salad servings or 12 relish servings

Carrot, Raisin & Pineapple Salad

Carrots combine ideally with pineapple and orange flavored yogurt for a light and colorful creation.

2½ cups shredded carrot
1 20-ounce can crushed pineapple, drained

½ cup raisins
1 cup Orange Yogurt Dressing

● Combine carrot, pineapple and raisins in a bowl. Toss with Orange Yogurt Dressing. ● Chill well before serving.

Yield: 6 servings

Cole Slaw

A pleasing addition to any meal. For an interesting variation, try a layer of Cole Slaw on your sandwich or burger.

1 large cabbage, shredded
2 carrots, shredded
½ cup chopped green bell pepper
¾ cup finely chopped onion

Marinade:
½ cup vinegar
¾ cup vegetable oil
2 tablespoons honey
2 tablespoons sugar
1 teaspoon salt

● Combine vegetables in a large bowl. ● Bring marinade ingredients to a boil in a saucepan. Pour boiling marinade over vegetables. Toss gently. ● Cover and chill.

Note: Make this at least 1 day in advance to allow the slaw to marinate. It can be stored in the refrigerator for up to 3 weeks. Drain excess liquid before serving.

Yield: 8 to 10 servings

Vinaigrette

Our version of France's most popular and traditional dressing.

¾ cup oil (half olive oil, half vegetable oil)
¼ cup vinegar
1 teaspoon prepared mustard
1 teaspoon salt

1 tablespoon mixed chopped fresh herbs (parsley, dill, chives, tarragon or basil) or ½ teaspoon dried
1 garlic clove, pressed
1 teaspoon honey (optional)

● Stir all ingredients together, mixing well. Shake well before serving.

Yield: 1 cup

Italian Salad Dressing

This versatile dressing is equally good on salads or when used as a marinade.

¾ cup olive oil (or half olive oil and half vegetable oil)
¼ cup vinegar
1 tablespoon minced fresh onion
1 garlic clove, crushed
1 teaspoon (scant) crumbled dry basil

1 teaspoon (scant) crumbled dry oregano
1 teaspoon honey (optional)
1 teaspoon salt
⅛ teaspoon freshly ground black pepper or to taste

● Combine all ingredients in a blender. Process until well mixed.

Yield: 1 cup

California Dressing

Zesty yet slightly sweet — this delightful dressing will add both color and flavor to your salads.

¾ cup vegetable oil
⅓ cup vinegar
¼ cup honey
2 tablespoons chopped onion
1 garlic clove, minced
3 tablespoons chili sauce
1 tablespoon fresh lemon juice

1 teaspoon powdered mustard
1 teaspoon salt
½ teaspoon crumbled dry basil
¼ teaspoon crumbled dry oregano
¼ teaspoon dried dill weed or 1 teaspoon chopped fresh dill

● Process all ingredients together in a blender or food processor until well mixed. ● Chill several hours before serving.

Yield: 1½ cups

Eggless Mayonnaise

This basic mayonnaise will be very useful in preparing a host of creamy dressings, sauces and sandwich spreads.

⅔ cup water
½ cup apple cider vinegar
2 tablespoons honey
1¼ teaspoons salt

½ teaspoon powdered mustard
1 tablespoon fresh lemon juice
1 cup non-instant milk powder
1½ cups mild-flavored vegetable oil

● Combine all ingredients except milk powder and vegetable oil in a blender. (Do not use a food processor — it does not produce the desired result for this recipe.) Blend until smooth.
● While blender is running, add the milk powder. *Keep blender running* while vegetable oil is added, pouring the oil in slowly, in a thin stream. ● Chill. Can be refrigerated in a covered container for up to 3 weeks.

Yield: 3½ cups

Thousand Island Dressing

Creamy, pink and popular.

1 cup Eggless Mayonnaise (above)
¼ cup chili sauce

1 tablespoon chopped green bell pepper
1 tablespoon minced fresh onion

● Stir all ingredients together, mixing well. Refrigerate.

Yield: 1⅓ cups

Russian Dressing

A renowned dressing that is so easy to prepare.

1 cup Eggless Mayonnaise (above)
¼ cup chili sauce
¼ cup relish

2 tablespoons milk
1 tablespoon fresh lemon juice
1 tablespoon minced fresh onion

● Stir all ingredients together, mixing well. Refrigerate.

Yield: 1⅔ cups

Creamy Italian Dressing

This dressing can transform an ordinary salad into a delectable one.

¾ cup Eggless Mayonnaise	2 teaspoons honey (optional)
¼ cup white vinegar	¾ teaspoon crumbled dry oregano
½ cup vegetable oil	½ teaspoon crumbled dry basil
2 tablespoons minced fresh onion	Salt to taste
1 garlic clove, minced	¼ to ½ cup milk

● Combine all ingredients except milk in a blender or food processor. Process until well mixed. Thin with milk to desired consistency. ● Chill before serving.

Yield: 1¾ cups

Creamy Surprise Dressing

Garnish romaine or iceberg lettuce salads with this rich and colorful dressing. Also good on cold sliced potatoes for a fast potato salad.

1 cup Eggless Mayonnaise	1 tablespoon chopped fresh chives
½ cup dairy sour cream	2 teaspoons fresh lemon juice
3 tablespoons chopped green or red bell pepper	1 teaspoon chopped fresh dill or ¼ teaspoon dried dill weed
2 tablespoons chopped fresh parsley	½ teaspoon paprika
3 tablespoons finely minced fresh onion	¼ teaspoon salt
2 tablespoons chopped pimento	⅛ teaspoon black pepper

● Stir all ingredients together, mixing thoroughly. Chill before serving.

Yield: 2 cups

Sesame Dressing

*There is nothing quite like the marvelous aroma and taste of freshly roasted sesame seeds —
the key ingredient in this unusual dressing.*

¼   **cup sesame seeds, unhulled preferred**
½   **cup light sesame or peanut oil**
1   **tablespoon vinegar**
2   **tablespoons fresh lemon juice**

2   **tablespoons tamari**
2   **garlic cloves, crushed or pressed**
⅛   **teaspoon cayenne pepper**

● Toast sesame seeds in an ungreased skillet over medium heat. Stir continuously until they begin to pop. Remove from heat and pour into a blender. ● Whirl in blender until powdered. Add all other ingredients and process until well blended. ● Store in refrigerator. Shake thoroughly before serving.

Yield: 1 cup

Tofu Dressing

*One marvel of protein-rich tofu is its great adaptability. The silken texture of soft tofu is ideal
for smooth, light dressings.*

½   **pound soft tofu**
1   **cup buttermilk**
1   **small garlic clove, pressed**
½   **cup Eggless Mayonnaise**
½   **teaspoon salt**

½   **teaspoon crumbled dry basil**
½   **teaspoon crumbled dry oregano**
½   **teaspoon dried parsley flakes**
⅛   **teaspoon black pepper**
1   **tablespoon lemon juice**

● Combine all ingredients in a blender or food processor. Whirl until well blended.
● Refrigerate, and use within 2 days for best flavor.

Yield: 2½ cups

Dressings

Greek Dressing

Generously seasoned with oregano, this tasty dressing will add life to a salad of vegetables, black olives and chunks of ripened cheese.

1 teaspoon agar flakes (not granules)	2 tablespoons chopped onion
½ cup water	2 tablespoons chopped fresh parsley
½ cup olive oil	Salt and pepper to taste
1½ teaspoons crumbled dry oregano	1 teaspoon chopped capers (optional)
3 tablespoons lemon juice	

● Combine agar and water in a small saucepan. Bring to a boil, then reduce heat and simmer for 10 minutes, stirring occasionally. Cool. ● Process cooled agar with all remaining ingredients except capers in a blender or food processor until well mixed. Stir in capers.
● Store in refrigerator. Use at room temperature (dressing thickens when chilled due to the olive oil). Shake before serving.

Yield: 1½ cups

Oriental Dressing

This appealing blend of flavors will highlight any vegetable salad.

½ cup light sesame or peanut oil	1 garlic clove, pressed
2 tablespoons fresh lemon juice	1 teaspoon brown sugar
1 tablespoon vinegar	1 teaspoon honey
2 tablespoons tamari	Pinch of cayenne pepper

● Stir all ingredients together, mixing well. Shake before serving.

Yield: ¾ cup

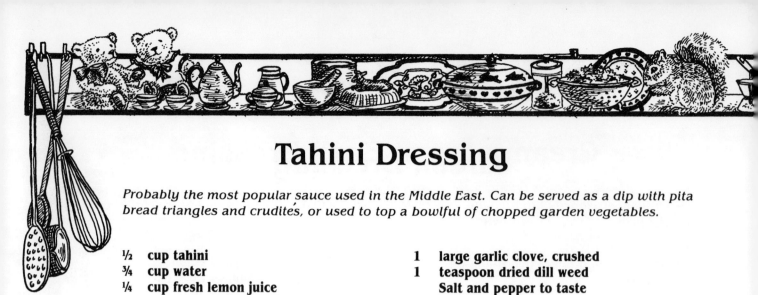

Tahini Dressing

Probably the most popular sauce used in the Middle East. Can be served as a dip with pita bread triangles and crudités, or used to top a bowlful of chopped garden vegetables.

½	cup tahini	1	large garlic clove, crushed
¾	cup water	1	teaspoon dried dill weed
¼	cup fresh lemon juice		Salt and pepper to taste

● Combine all ingredients in a blender or food processor. Whirl until smooth. Refrigerate.

Yield: 1½ cups

Walnut Dressing

This distinctive dressing from Turkey is particularly tasty on cold, cooked vegetables.

1	cup chopped walnuts	¼	cup (packed) chopped fresh parsley or mint
1	large garlic clove	2	medium-sized scallions, chopped
¼	cup dry bread crumbs	½	teaspoon salt
1	cup milk		Cayenne pepper to taste
4	tablespoons fresh lemon juice	1	teaspoon honey (optional)

● Whirl walnuts, garlic and bread crumbs in blender or food processor. Add other ingredients and process thoroughly. Add a little more milk if thinner consistency is desired. ● Store in refrigerator.

Yield: 2½ cups

Avocado Dressing

A chili-spiced dressing which can double as a dip for crisp tortilla chips. For added zip be generous with the hot pepper sauce.

½	cup chopped avocado	1	small garlic clove
½	cup dairy sour cream	½	teaspoon (scant) chili powder
1	to 2 tablespoons fresh lemon juice	¼	teaspoon salt
⅓	cup vegetable oil	¼	teaspoon hot pepper sauce or to taste
1	tablespoon chopped onion		

● Process all ingredients in a blender or food processor until puréed. Place in a container with a cover (along with the avocado pit, which will help prevent discoloration). ● Can be refrigerated for up to 3 days. The flavor improves with an hour or more of chilling.

Yield: 1½ cups

Dressings

Creamy Fresh Basil Dressing

The beautiful fragrance and unique taste of basil provide a special touch to summer salads.

12	large fresh basil leaves
8	ounces cream cheese, at room temperature
½	cup water
1	tablespoon lemon juice
1	teaspoon tamari
1	small garlic clove

2	tablespoons chopped onion
	Freshly ground black pepper to taste
	Salt to taste
2	tablespoons grated Parmesan cheese (optional)
2	tablespoons chopped red onion (optional)

● Wash basil leaves well. Combine basil with all ingredients except red onion in a blender or food processor. Whirl until well blended. ● Stir in red onion. Refrigerate.

Note: If you like the tangy taste of basil to predominate, 12 leaves are only a beginning. Add more, *a little at a time,* when increasing the amount. Fresh basil is preferred for this dressing, but when it is not available, substitute 1 tablespoon crumbled dry basil.

Yield: 1½ cups

Blue Cheese Dressing

For a classic salad, serve a wedge of crisp, cold iceberg lettuce surrounded by sliced tomatoes, and top it with our mellow Blue Cheese Dressing.

4	ounces blue cheese, crumbled
½	cup Eggless Mayonnaise
½	cup dairy sour cream
¼	cup milk

2	tablespoons fresh lemon juice
1	tablespoon finely chopped onion
2	teaspoons sugar or honey (optional)
	Dash of hot pepper sauce

● Stir all ingredients together, mixing thoroughly. Refrigerate.

Yield: 1⅔ cups

Lemon & Lime Fruit Dressing

A refreshing citrus favorite for both summer and winter fruit salads.

½   cup dairy sour cream
½   cup unflavored yogurt
2   tablespoons mild-flavored honey
2   tablespoons sugar

2   tablespoons fresh lemon juice
2   tablespoons fresh lime juice
1   teaspoon grated lemon peel

● Stir all ingredients together, mixing thoroughly. Refrigerate until well chilled.

Yield: 1½ cups

Curried Mango Dressing

The subtle flavor of mangoes combines with curry and ginger to produce an interesting fruit salad topping. Particularly tasty over sliced fresh peaches and blueberries.

1   tablespoon butter
¼   teaspoon grated fresh ginger root
1   teaspoon curry powder

½   cup ripe mango pulp
2   tablespoons honey
1   cup unflavored yogurt

● Melt butter in a small skillet. Sauté grated ginger and curry powder in butter for a few minutes over low heat. ● Add mango and honey and continue cooking a few more minutes. Set aside to cool. ● When cooled, stir in yogurt. Spoon over sliced or chopped fruit.

Yield: 1½ cups

Fresh Peach Dressing

This delightful dressing is outstanding on fresh fruits and berries. Good with ice cream too!

½   pound fresh peaches, chopped
     (about 1½ cups)
¼   cup dairy sour cream or unflavored
     yogurt

2   tablespoons honey
¼   teaspoon freshly grated ginger

● Combine all ingredients together in a blender or food processor. Whirl until smooth.
● Refrigerate.

Yield: 1¼ cups

Orange Yogurt Dressing

Especially appealing on fresh fruit salads.

1	cup unflavored yogurt	½	teaspoon grated orange peel
2	tablespoons orange juice concentrate, undiluted	2	teaspoons honey

● Stir all ingredients together, mixing well. Refrigerate.

Yield: 1 cup

Lo-Cal Yogurt Dressing

Cool, creamy and flavorful.

2	cups unflavored yogurt	½	teaspoon salt or to taste
2	tablespoons minced fresh mint or 1 teaspoon dried	¾	teaspoon ground cumin Freshly ground black pepper

● Stir yogurt together with all other ingredients. Serve over vegetable salads.

Yield: 2 cups

Bread

Coffee Cakes, Muffins & Such

Irish Soda Bread

Our version of Ireland's popular quick bread, with its unique combination of currants and caraway seeds, is delicious served with butter and preserves.

5	cups unbleached white flour or half whole wheat flour	1	tablespoon baking powder
1	cup sugar	3	tablespoons caraway seeds
1½	teaspoons salt	½	cup butter, melted
1	teaspoon baking soda	2½	cups buttermilk
		2½	cups currants

● Combine the first six ingredients in a mixing bowl. Add melted butter and buttermilk and mix well. Stir in currants. Mixture will be sticky. ● Spoon into a greased 9 × 13-inch baking pan (or two 9 × 5-inch loaf pans). Bake at 350° F. for about 1 hour.

Yield: 16 servings

Cornbread

This American specialty from our Southern states has real down-home flavor. Especially good served with chili or any bean dish for a complete protein meal.

1	cup cornmeal	1	teaspoon salt
½	cup whole wheat flour	1⅓	cups milk
½	cup unbleached white flour	2	tablespoons honey
2	teaspoons baking powder	⅓	cup vegetable oil or melted butter

● Sift dry ingredients together. Add remaining ingredients, stirring just until moistened.
● Pour batter into a greased 9-inch pie plate or 8-inch square pan. Bake at 425° F. for 25 minutes or until top is golden and firm.

Yield: 6 servings

Quick Cinnamon Raisin Bread

The appealing blend of raisins and spice is the hallmark of this fragrant quick bread.

2	cups whole wheat flour	½	teaspoon ground nutmeg
1	teaspoon baking powder	½	teaspoon ground ginger
1	teaspoon baking soda	¼	cup butter
1	teaspoon salt	½	cup honey
1	teaspoon dry egg replacer	1¾	cups vanilla flavored yogurt
1	teaspoon ground cinnamon	¾	cup raisins

● In a large mixing bowl, combine the first 8 ingredients. ● Melt butter in a small saucepan. Remove from heat and stir in honey and yogurt. Add to dry ingredients and mix lightly, just until combined. ● Stir in raisins. Bake in a greased 9 × 5-inch loaf pan at 350° F. for 50 to 60 minutes. ● Remove from pan and let cool on a wire rack before slicing.

Yield: one 9 × 5-inch loaf

Cranberry Nut Bread

This richly colored bread, with its tangy, sweet flavor, will brighten any holiday meal and is beautiful enough for gift giving.

½ cup whole wheat flour	1 tablespoon grated orange rind
1½ cups unbleached white flour	¾ cup orange juice
1 cup sugar	2 tablespoons butter, at room temperature
1½ teaspoons baking powder	1 cup fresh whole cranberries
1 teaspoon baking soda	½ cup chopped pecans or walnuts
1 teaspoon salt	

● Combine flours, sugar, baking powder, baking soda and salt in a medium-sized bowl. Stir to mix well. ● Add orange rind, orange juice and butter. Mix thoroughly. Fold in cranberries and pecans or walnuts. Batter will be thick. ● Bake in a buttered 9 × 5-inch loaf pan at 350° F. for about 1 hour. Let cool 10 minutes in pan, then remove from pan and place on a wire rack. Let cool completely before slicing.

Yield: one 9 × 5-inch loaf

Banana Nut Bread

The marvelous flavor of bananas permeates this popular cake-like loaf. Slice thinly and spread with cream cheese or fruit butter for a lunch box or teatime treat.

1 cup whole wheat flour	¼ cup butter, melted
1 cup unbleached white flour	1 cup chopped walnuts
¾ cup sugar (see note)	1½ cups mashed ripe banana
1 tablespoon baking powder	¼ cup buttermilk or milk soured with
½ teaspoon baking soda	½ teaspoon lemon juice
½ teaspoon salt	2 teaspoons vanilla extract

● In a large mixing bowl, sift together flours, sugar, baking powder, baking soda and salt. ● Combine melted butter, walnuts, mashed banana, buttermilk or soured milk and vanilla extract. Add to dry ingredients, mixing just until well moistened. ● Turn into a greased 9 × 5-inch loaf pan. Smooth top. Bake at 350° F. for 1 hour. ● Let stand in pan 10 minutes, then remove and cool on a wire rack. Let cool completely before slicing.

Note: To use honey instead of sugar, substitute ½ cup honey for the sugar and omit the buttermilk or soured milk.

Yield: one 9 × 5-inch loaf

Sweet Yeast Dough

You will find this is a versatile dough that adapts wonderfully for coffee cakes, breads or rolls.

2 packages active dry yeast
½ cup warm water (110° F.)
½ cup warm milk (110° F.)
½ cup sugar or honey

1 teaspoon salt
½ cup butter, at room temperature
4½ cups (about) unbleached white flour

● In a large mixing bowl, dissolve yeast in warm water. Add milk, sugar or honey, salt, butter and half of the flour. Beat until smooth. Mix in enough remaining flour to make the dough easy to handle. ● Turn dough onto a floured surface. Knead 5 to 10 minutes until smooth and elastic. ● Place in a greased bowl, then turn dough greased-side up. Cover with a clean towel. Let rise in a warm place until doubled in bulk, about 1½ hours. Punch down. ● Shape into rolls or use for coffee cakes. ● Let rise until doubled in bulk, about 30 minutes. Bake in greased pans at 375° for 25 to 35 minutes. Allow more time for larger shapes, less for smaller shapes.

Yield: dough for one large or two small coffee cakes

Viennese Coffee Cake

This Viennese creation boasts a sweet yeast dough wrapped around a savory apple or almond filling.

Sweet Yeast Dough
Apple Filling:
4 medium-sized apples, pared and thinly sliced
½ cup chopped pecans or walnuts
½ cup raisins
2 tablespoons sugar
1 teaspoon ground cinnamon

Almond Filling:
½ cup butter, at room temperature
¼ cup sugar
2 teaspoons vanilla extract
½ teaspoon ground cinnamon
1 cup slivered almonds
1 cup raisins
½ cup golden raisins

● After first rising of Sweet Yeast Dough, punch dough down. Roll on a floured surface to form one large ½-inch thick rectangle, or two smaller ones. ● If using Apple Filling, toss filling ingredients together until well mixed. For Almond Filling, first cream butter and sugar, then mix in remaining ingredients. ● Spread filling mixture over one half of the rectangle, leaving a ½-inch border of dough around all edges for sealing. Fold in half lengthwise. Press edges with a fork to seal tightly. ● Place on a greased cookie sheet. Let rise in a warm place until doubled in bulk, about 30 minutes. ● Bake at 375° F. for about 25 minutes or until golden brown.

Yield: 1 large or 2 small coffee cakes

Breads

Pecan Coffee Cake

A delectable, tender coffee cake.

1½ cups unbleached white flour or half
       whole wheat pastry flour
2 teaspoons baking powder
½ teaspoon salt
¾ cup brown sugar
¼ cup butter, melted
½ cup milk
½ teaspoon vanilla extract

Topping:
½ cup brown sugar
2 tablespoons butter, melted
1 tablespoon unbleached white flour
1 teaspoon ground cinnamon
1 cup chopped pecans

● Sift flour with baking powder and salt. Mix in sugar, melted butter, milk and vanilla extract.
● Prepare topping by combining all topping ingredients in order given. ● Press half of batter over the bottom of a greased 8-inch square baking pan. Sprinkle half the topping over this. Dot with remaining batter. Moisten fingertips with water and smooth batter to cover brown sugar mixture. Sprinkle with remaining topping. ● Bake at 350° F. for about 30 minutes until done.

Yield: 6 servings

Wheat & Honey Bread

If you are new at bread-making, try our excellent Wheat and Honey Bread for loaves you can be proud of.

2 packages active dry yeast
½ cup warm water (110° F.)
⅓ cup honey or sugar
¼ cup melted butter

1 tablespoon salt
1¾ cups warm water (110° F.)
3 cups whole wheat flour
3 to 4 cups unbleached white flour

● Dissolve yeast in ½ cup warm water in a large mixing bowl. Add honey or sugar, melted butter, salt, 1¾ cups warm water and the whole wheat flour. Beat until smooth. ● Mix in white flour until dough is easy to handle. Turn dough onto a floured surface and knead for about 10 minutes until smooth and elastic. Place in a large greased bowl and cover with a light cloth. Let rise until doubled in bulk, about 1 hour. ● Punch dough down and let rise again until doubled in bulk. ● Punch down and divide in half. Form into loaves and place in two greased 9 × 5-inch loaf pans. (Round loaves can be shaped and placed directly on greased baking sheets.) Let rise until doubled in bulk, about 45 minutes. ● Bake at 375° F. for 40 to 45 minutes or until golden brown. When done, loaves should sound hollow when tapped on the bottom. Let cool on wire racks.

Note: These loaves should rise nicely in the oven during baking. Be sure to place them on a lower-middle rack to allow them plenty of room.

Yield: two 9 × 5-inch loaves

100% Whole Wheat Bread

A wholesome grain bread with an even texture, which makes it ideal for sandwiches or toast.

2	packages active dry yeast	¼	cup honey
1	cup warm water (110° F.)	¼	cup molasses
2	cups warm milk (110° F.)	1	tablespoon salt
¼	cup vegetable oil	8	cups whole wheat flour

● Combine yeast and water in a large mixing bowl. Set aside for a few minutes. ● Stir together milk, vegetable oil, honey, molasses and salt. Add to yeast and stir. Mix in half the flour and stir until smooth. Beat for 3 minutes. Gradually add remaining flour, mixing until dough is workable. ● Turn onto a floured surface. Knead for 10 minutes until smooth and springy. Place in an oiled bowl and let rise until doubled in bulk, about 1 hour. ● Punch dough down and let rise again until doubled. ● Punch down and divide into 3 equal portions. Form into loaves. Place in three greased 9 × 5-inch loaf pans. Let rise for 30 to 40 minutes until almost doubled in bulk. ● Bake at 425° F. for 15 minutes. Reduce heat to 350° F. and bake for 30 minutes or until done. For a soft crust, brush top with butter or vegetable oil after removing from oven. Let cool on wire racks.

Yield: three 9 × 5-inch loaves

Sesame Oatmeal Bread

Full-bodied and chewy, with flavorful goodness in every bite.

1	cup old-fashioned rolled oats	½	cup wheat germ
2	cups water	½	cup vegetable oil
¾	cup sesame seeds, hulled or unhulled		*Glaze:*
1	tablespoon active dry yeast	½	teaspoon cornstarch
1½	cups warm water (110° F.)	¼	cup water
¾	cup honey	1	tablespoon toasted sesame
5	to 6 cups whole wheat flour		seeds (reserved)
1	tablespoon salt		

● Cook oats in 2 cups water according to package instructions. Set aside to cool to lukewarm. ● Meanwhile, toast sesame seeds over medium heat in an ungreased skillet until lightly browned, stirring frequently. Set aside. ● Dissolve yeast in warm water in a large mixing bowl. Add honey, toasted sesame seeds (reserve 1 tablespoon for glaze) and oatmeal. Mix in 2 cups of flour. Beat about 100 times to develop the gluten. Cover with a clean damp cloth. Let rise in a warm place for 40 minutes. ● Stir in salt, wheat germ, vegetable oil and 3 more cups of flour. Turn onto a floured smooth surface and knead, using additional flour as necessary, until soft and elastic. Place dough in a lightly greased bowl and let rise 1 hour. Punch down. Let rise again for 40 minutes. ● Knead dough gently. Divide in half and form into two loaves. Place in greased 9 × 5-inch loaf pans. Let rise in a warm place for 20 to 30 minutes. Bake at 350° F. for 50 to 70 minutes. Ten minutes before baking is completed, prepare the Glaze. Stir cornstarch into cold water in a small saucepan. Bring to a boil, cook and stir for 1 minute until thickened. Remove breads from oven at once and brush with mixture. Sprinkle reserved sesame seeds on top of each loaf. Return to oven for remainder of baking time. ● Remove from pans and cool on wire racks before slicing.

Yield: two 9 × 5-inch loaves

Breads

Rye Bread

Moist and full of hearty rye flavor.

1½ cups whole wheat flour
2½ cups unbleached white flour
2   packages active dry yeast
1   tablespoon caraway seeds
1   teaspoon salt

2   cups warm water (110° F.)
½   cup honey
1   tablespoon vegetable oil
2½ cups rye flour

● Combine whole wheat flour, 1 cup of the unbleached white flour, yeast, caraway seeds and salt in a large mixing bowl. ● Add water, honey and vegetable oil. Beat at low speed for one minute, then beat for 3 minutes at high speed. Stir in rye flour and as much of the remaining 1½ cups unbleached white flour as you can. ● Turn onto a floured surface and knead about 8 minutes for a moderately stiff dough. Form into a ball and place in a greased bowl. Cover and let rise about 1½ hours or until doubled in bulk. ● Punch dough down. Divide in half and let rest 10 minutes. Shape into two 4- to 5-inch round loaves. Place on greased baking sheets. Let rise about 30 minutes until nearly doubled in bulk. ● Bake at 350° F. for 40 to 45 minutes. Cool on wire racks.

Yield: 2 round loaves

Orange Rye Bread

A light and aromatic loaf.

2   packages active dry yeast
2   cups warm water (110° F.)
½   cup sugar
1   tablespoon salt
2   teaspoons grated orange peel

2   teaspoons caraway seeds
2   tablespoons vegetable oil
2   cups rye flour
4   cups unbleached white flour

● Dissolve yeast in water in a large mixing bowl. Add sugar, salt, orange peel, caraway seeds and vegetable oil. Stir in half the flour and mix well. ● Add remaining flour and mix with your hands. Turn dough onto a lightly floured surface and knead about 10 minutes until smooth and elastic. ● Form into a ball. Place in a large oiled bowl and turn dough to coat with oil. Cover with a damp cloth and let rise in a warm place for 1 to 2 hours until doubled in bulk. ● Punch down dough. Let rise again for 45 minutes. ● Punch down again and divide in half. Form into round loaves and place on greased baking sheets. Let rise until doubled in bulk, about 1 hour. ● Bake at 375° F. for 15 minutes. Reduce heat to 350° F. and bake about 30 more minutes until done. ● Cool on wire racks. For a soft crust, rub butter over top of bread while bread is still hot. Cool completely before slicing.

Yield: two 9 x 5-inch loaves

Anadama Bread

The traditional combination of cornmeal and molasses makes this Early American bread a perennial favorite.

2 tablespoons active dry yeast	½ cup light molasses
½ cup warm water (110° F.)	2 teaspoons salt
¼ cup butter, cut into chunks	¾ cup milk
1 cup boiling water	2 cups whole wheat flour
¾ cup cornmeal	4½ to 5½ cups unbleached white flour

● Sprinkle yeast into warm water in a small bowl. Stir to dissolve. Let stand 5 minutes. ● In a large mixing bowl, combine butter, boiling water, cornmeal, molasses and salt. Mix well. When butter has melted, stir in milk. When mixture has cooled to lukewarm, stir in dissolved yeast. ● Mix in all the whole wheat flour and 2 cups of the unbleached white flour. Beat at medium speed for 2 minutes. Stir in 2 more cups of white flour. ● Turn dough onto a well floured smooth surface. Knead for about 10 minutes, adding additional flour as needed until dough is smooth and elastic. ● Place in a greased bowl. Cover and let rise in a warm place for about 1 hour until doubled in bulk. Punch down. Let rise again until doubled. ● Punch down and divide dough in half. Shape into loaves. Place in two well buttered 9 × 5-inch loaf pans. ● Cover with a damp cloth and let rise about 30 minutes or until almost doubled in bulk. Place in a cold oven. Set temperature at 375° F. and bake for 30 minutes. Reduce heat to 350° F. and bake another 10 minutes or until done. Loaves should sound hollow when tapped on the bottoms. ● Let cool on wire racks before slicing.

Yield: two 9 × 5-inch loaves

Swirled Apricot Bread

A sumptuous whole wheat bread swirled with tangy apricots, crunchy nuts and cinnamon.

3½ cups whole wheat flour	⅓ cup vegetable oil
½ cup wheat germ	⅓ cup honey
2 packages active dry yeast	2½ to 3 cups unbleached white flour
1 teaspoon salt	2 cups chopped walnuts
1 teaspoon ground cinnamon	2 cups finely snipped dried apricots
2½ cups milk	

● Combine 2½ cups of the whole wheat flour with the wheat germ, yeast, salt and cinnamon in a large bowl of an electric mixer. ● In a small saucepan, heat milk, vegetable oil and honey over low heat until very warm (120° to 130° F.). Gradually add warm liquid to dry ingredients in mixer at low speed. Increase to medium speed and beat 3 minutes. ● Mix in remaining 1 cup whole wheat flour and 1 cup of the unbleached white flour. Beat with a dough hook for 5 minutes at slow speed or use a wooden spoon. Mix in chopped walnuts. ● Gradually add 1½ cups unbleached white flour. Turn onto a well floured smooth surface. Knead about 10 minutes until dough is no longer sticky. Add flour as needed. ● Divide dough into two portions. Let rest 15 minutes. ● With a rolling pin, roll each portion into a 9 × 16-inch rectangle. Sprinkle half the fruit over each rectangle. Roll dough tightly in jelly-roll fashion from the 9-inch end. Place each loaf seam side down in a well greased 9 × 5-inch loaf pan. Cover with a light towel and let rise until doubled in bulk, about 1 hour. ● Bake at 375° F. for about 40 minutes or until tops are nicely browned and bottoms sound hollow when tapped.

Yield: 2 loaves

French Bread

An outstanding classic, this French Bread with its fine crust will grace any table.

2	packages active dry yeast
½	cup warm water (110° F.)
2	teaspoons sugar or honey

5	cups unbleached white flour
2	teaspoons salt
1½	cups additional warm water

● In a large mixing bowl, dissolve yeast in ½ cup warm water with sugar or honey. Set aside for 5 to 10 minutes until yeast begins to foam. ● Add 2 cups of the unbleached white flour, salt and additional water. Beat at medium speed for one minute. Add remaining flour and beat on low speed for 2 minutes, scraping the sides of the bowl from time to time. Let dough rest for 5 minutes. ● Turn dough onto a lightly floured smooth surface. Knead at least 20 minutes until smooth and elastic. (Long kneading is necessary for classic French bread texture.) Place dough in a lightly greased bowl, turning to grease top of dough. Cover bowl with a damp cloth. Let rise in a warm place until doubled in size, about 1 hour. ● Punch dough down. Let rise an additional hour. ● Divide dough into 2 pieces for large full-sized loaves, or into 4 pieces for narrow baquette loaves. Roll each section into a rope about 15-inches long. Place in special French bread pans which have been lightly oiled and sprinkled with cornmeal, or place on greased baking sheets which have been sprinkled with cornmeal. Let rise in a warm place for 1 to 1½ hours or until almost doubled in bulk. With a sharp knife, make 5 diagonal slashes across the top of each loaf, or one long surface cut down the center of loaf. ● Bake at 450° F. for 20 to 25 minutes, allowing a little extra baking time for larger loaves. For a nice crunchy crust, place a pan of water on the oven rack below the loaves before heating oven. Also, brush the tops of the loaves with cold water just before baking, then again at 5 minutes and 10 minutes after placing in oven.

Note: For **Whole Wheat French Bread**, use 3 cups whole wheat flour, 2 cups unbleached white flour and 1 tablespoon salt.

Yield: 2 large or 4 small loaves

Scones

Try these wedge-shaped Scottish biscuits which are perfect for a light luncheon or with tea.

1	cup buttermilk
2	tablespoons honey
2½	cups unbleached white flour
1	cup whole wheat flour
2	teaspoons baking powder

1	teaspoon baking soda
½	teaspoon salt
½	cup melted butter
⅓	cup dried currants

● Combine buttermilk and honey in a mixing bowl. ● Sift the flours with baking powder, baking soda and salt. Stir about ⅔ of the flour mixture into the buttermilk. Slowly mix in the melted butter. Lightly stir in remaining flour. Add currants. ● Turn onto a floured surface and knead the dough gently for a few minutes. Divide into three equal sections. Gently flatten dough to form thick rounds about 4 to 5 inches in diameter. With a sharp knife, quarter the rounds into 4 wedges each. ● Place scones ½ inch apart on a buttered cookie sheet. Bake at 375° F. for 15 to 20 minutes or until golden. Serve warm with butter and strawberry or currant jam.

Yield: 12 scones

Whole Wheat Dinner Rolls

These tender, light rolls are sure crowd-pleasers. Have fun experimenting with the variety of shapes offered or try creating your own.

2 **cups milk**	1 **tablespoon salt**
2 **packages active dry yeast**	3 **cups whole wheat flour**
½ **cup warm water (110° F.)**	5 **cups (about) unbleached white flour**
½ **cup sugar**	**Melted, unsalted butter for brushing**
6 **tablespoons vegetable oil**	

● Gently heat milk to warm (110° F.). ● Meanwhile, dissolve yeast in a small bowl with ½ cup warm water and one teaspoon of the sugar. Set aside for about 10 minutes until yeast begins to foam. ● In a large mixing bowl, combine remaining sugar, vegetable oil, salt and the warm milk. Add yeast mixture. Stir in 2 cups whole wheat flour and 2 cups unbleached white flour. Beat on low speed for 2 minutes, then beat on high for 2 minutes. ● Return to low speed and add remaining 1 cup whole wheat flour and 1 more cup white flour. Beat one minute. Work in remaining flour by hand. Let dough rest for 5 minutes. ● Turn dough onto a lightly floured smooth surface. Knead for 10 minutes or until smooth and elastic, using additional white flour as needed. Shape into a ball and place in a large greased bowl, turning the dough over to grease top. Cover with a damp cloth and let rise in a warm place for about 1 hour or until doubled in bulk. ● Punch dough down. Let rise 1 more hour. Punch down again. Turn dough onto a lightly floured surface and form into desired shapes. (See instructions below.) ● For baking, position rolls roughly 1 inch apart on greased baking sheets or in muffin tins. Brush with melted, unsalted butter and allow to rise in a warm place for 20 to 30 minutes until puffed. ● Bake at 375° F. for 15 to 20 minutes until browned.

Yield: 3 to 4 dozen

Cloverleaf Rolls: Roll out a portion of the dough by hand into a coil 1 inch thick. Break off pieces of the coil and roll in palms to form balls 1 inch in diameter. Place 3 balls side by side in well greased muffin tins.

Accordian Rolls: Roll out dough to form a rectangle ¼ inch thick. Brush with melted butter. Cut into strips 1½ inches wide. Stack seven strips together and cut into 1½-inch squares. Place each stack on its side (cut-side up) in well greased muffin tins.

Crescent Rolls: On a lightly floured surface, roll dough out to form 9-inch circles, ¼ inch thick. Slice into 8 wedges. Brush tops with melted, unsalted butter. Starting at the wide end, roll each wedge, then curve ends to form a crescent. Seal tip. Brush with butter again and place tip-side down, 1 inch apart, on well greased baking sheets.

Knot Rolls: Roll dough out to form a rectangle ¼ inch thick. Slice into strips ½ inch wide and roughly 5 inches long. Roll the strips by hand to round and lengthen each piece. Brush with melted, unsalted butter. Twist each "rope" and tie into a knot. Brush with butter again. Place knot-side up, 1 inch apart, on well greased baking sheets.

Coil Rolls: Follow same procedure as for Knot Rolls. Once each strip is rounded and lengthened, brush with butter, then wrap it around your index finger to form a flat coil. (It is easiest to do this directly on well greased baking sheets.) Brush with butter again.

Braids: Roll out dough into a rectangle ¼ inch thick. Cut into strips ½ inch wide and 7 to 8 inches long. Roll by hand to round and gently stretch each strip. Take 3 rounded strips and begin to braid from the center. (Start in middle and braid towards one end, pinching ends to seal. Then braid towards other end.) Tuck ends under and place at least 1 inch apart on well greased baking sheets.

Water Bagels

Once found only in ethnic bakeries, bagels are now popular throughout the world. These homemade bagels have a wonderful crust and are delicious when toasted and served with butter or cream cheese, or when filled with one of your favorite sandwich spreads.

1	package active dry yeast	
1½	cups warm water (110° F.)	
2	tablespoons sugar or powdered whey	
¾	tablespoon salt	
4	cups (about) high-gluten white bread flour	

Sesame seeds or poppy seeds (optional)
Water Bath:
2 quarts water
1 tablespoon sugar

● Sprinkle yeast into warm water in a large bowl and stir gently. Add sugar or whey and continue to stir until dissolved. Mix in salt and flour. Work the dough with your hands, kneading until a stiff dough is formed. ● Turn dough onto a floured surface and knead until smooth. Shape dough into a ball and place in an ungreased bowl. Cover with plastic wrap and let rise in a warm place until doubled in bulk, about 1½ to 2 hours. ● Bring Water Bath ingredients to a boil in a large pot. Meanwhile, punch dough down and divide into 10 equal portions. Form into the shape of doughnuts with an elongated center hole about 1 inch across. (An easy method is to make a flat round, then poke a hole in center with fingers.) Do not make bagels too rounded in height as they will puff up further when baked. ● When water comes to a boil, turn heat off. As boiling subsides, slip a few bagels in. Cook for 20 seconds on each side. Immediately lift bagels from water using a slotted spoon. Drain briefly on paper towels. Repeat for remaining bagels. ● If sesame or poppy seed bagels are desired, spread seeds on a plate and press one or both sides of bagel into seeds after draining. Place bagels on two greased cookie sheets. ● Bake at 450° F. for 10 to 15 minutes. Turn bagels with a spatula and bake another 10 to 15 minutes until golden brown. Slice bagels across, through the middle, before serving. Serve warm or toasted with cream cheese, butter, preserves or your favorite spread.

Yield: 10 bagels

Oatcakes

In Great Britain, crisp, thin oatcakes are usually served with butter and preserves or cheese.

1	cup quick-cooking rolled oats	⅛	teaspoon salt	
½	cup unbleached white flour	6	tablespoons butter, at room temperature	
½	cup whole wheat flour	3	to 4 tablespoons cold water	

● Combine rolled oats, flours and salt. Cut butter into dry ingredients until coarse textured. Add water, one tablespoon at a time, to form a dough that just holds together. Add a little more water if necessary. ● Turn onto a lightly floured smooth surface. Roll to ⅛-inch thickness. Cut into 2½-inch squares or use a cookie cutter to cut into 3-inch circles, then slice in half to form semicircles. ● Bake on an ungreased cookie sheet at 375° F. for 12 to 15 minutes or until lightly browned. ● Cool on wire racks. Store in a tightly sealed container to retain crispness.

Yield: about 16 oatcakes

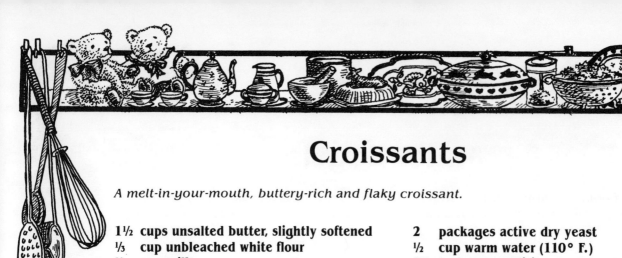

Croissants

A melt-in-your-mouth, buttery-rich and flaky croissant.

1½ cups unsalted butter, slightly softened
⅓ cup unbleached white flour
¾ cup milk
¼ cup sugar
1 teaspoon salt

2 packages active dry yeast
½ cup warm water (110° F.)
3½ to 4 cups additional unbleached white flour

● Cream butter with ⅓ cup flour. Spoon out creamed butter onto a sheet of waxed paper to form a rectangle about 4 × 10 inches. Cover with another sheet of waxed paper and roll out butter to form a 6 × 12-inch rectangle. Refrigerate for at least one hour. ● Combine milk, sugar and salt in a saucepan. Gently heat to warm (110° F.) temperature. Meanwhile, dissolve yeast in ½ cup warm water in a large mixing bowl. Let stand for 5 to 10 minutes until foamy. ● Stir warm milk into yeast. Add 2 cups flour and mix well. Stir in as much of the remaining flour as can be mixed in with a wooden spoon. ● Turn dough onto a lightly floured smooth surface. Knead for 10 minutes or until dough is smooth and elastic, adding flour as needed. Place in a bowl and cover with a light towel. Let dough rest for 10 minutes. ● Roll out dough on a lightly floured surface to a 14-inch square. Remove butter from refrigerator and place on one half of the square. Fold over other half of dough to enclose the butter. *Seal edges well.* Roll out to form a 12 × 21-inch rectangle. Fold the dough into thirds by overlapping ends. Seal edges. Cover and refrigerate for 30 to 45 minutes. ● Remove from refrigerator and roll out again to a 12 × 21-inch rectangle. Fold in thirds and refrigerate again for 30 to 45 minutes. *Repeat process two more times.* For the final chilling, refrigerate for *several hours or overnight.* ● Remove dough from refrigerator. Place on a lightly floured surface. Cut widthwise into thirds. Take each section and press it with the palm of your hand to form a circular shape, then roll into a 12-inch circle. Cut each circle into 8 wedges. Roll up each wedge, starting with the wide end. Place croissants point-side down on ungreased baking sheets (leave room for rising of dough). Curve ends to form a crescent shape. ● Let rise in a warm place for 1 to 2 hours until doubled in bulk. Bake at 375° F. for 12 to 15 minutes until golden. Serve warm.

Note: For larger croissants which can be sliced in half and used with sandwich fillings, roll dough in final process to a 16-inch circle. Cut into 4 wedges instead of 8.

Yield: 2 dozen

African Cheese Puffs

Biscuits with a tangy bite.

1 cup unbleached white flour or whole wheat pastry flour
2 teaspoons baking powder
1 teaspoon salt

½ teaspoon powdered mustard
½ teaspoon black pepper
¾ cup milk
1¼ cups shredded Cheddar or jack cheese

● Sift first five ingredients together. ● Stir in milk, mixing just until well moistened. Add cheese and stir lightly. ● Spoon batter into well greased and floured 2½-inch muffin tins. Bake at 350° F. for about 25 minutes. Serve warm with butter.

Yield: 1 dozen

Breads

Chapatis

A chewy, flat round of whole wheat bread that is traditionally served at every Indian meal.

2   cups whole wheat flour   **1   cup water**

● Place flour in a bowl. Make a well in the center of the flour and add water gradually, mixing until a soft dough is formed. ● Turn onto a lightly floured smooth surface. Knead the dough a few minutes until it is pliable. Cover with a damp cloth and let stand at least 30 minutes. ● Form dough into 12 balls. Flatten on a lightly floured surface to form even rounds, 2 or 3 inches in diameter. Roll each round out to form a 6-inch circle. ● Cook chapatis one at a time on a hot, oiled chapati griddle or a heavy skillet over medium-high heat. When the underside is lightly browned, flip the chapati. Press the top side of the chapati firmly with a clean towel or cloth napkin in several places, covering the entire surface. The chapati will puff up irregularly as it is cooked and pressed. ● Transfer to a hot platter when cooked.

Note: Chapati flour is available in Indian grocery stores, but regular whole wheat flour may be substituted with similar results.

Yield: 1 dozen

Puris

These delicate puffs of deep-fried bread make a wonderful accompaniment to an Indian dinner.

1   cup whole wheat flour   **⅓   cup water**
1   tablespoon vegetable oil   **Vegetable oil for deep-frying**

● Sift flour. Combine flour, 1 tablespoon vegetable oil and water together, mixing well. Knead on a lightly floured smooth surface for a few minutes. Place in a bowl and cover with a damp cloth. Let stand at least 1 hour. ● Form dough into balls 1 inch in diameter. Oil a rolling pin and oil a smooth working area. Don't use flour! Roll out each ball to form as smooth a circle as possible, 3 to 3½ inches in diameter. ● Slip a few puris at a time into hot vegetable oil (375° F.). As they rise to the surface, use a slotted spatula to gently push puris down, holding them just under the oil. At this point the puris should puff up. Turn to brown both sides. ● Remove from oil with a spatula and drain on paper towels. Serve at once while hot.

Yield: about 1 dozen

Fruit Muffins

Here is a wholesome and naturally sweet muffin, chock-full of fruit.

1 cup chopped pitted dates or other dried fruit
2 cups uncooked old-fashioned rolled oats
1 cup shredded coconut (optional)
2 teaspoons baking powder
¼ teaspoon salt

½ cup vegetable oil
3 cups crushed fruit with pulp and juice (strawberries, pineapple, whole blueberries)
1 tablespoon vanilla extract
2 or more cups whole wheat flour

● Combine all ingredients except flour and mix well. Stir in flour, using a little more or less depending upon the juiciness of the fruit. Batter should be thick but moist. ● Fill greased muffin tins (mixture will not rise much). Bake at 350° F. for about 50 minutes or until firm to the touch. Let stand in tins for 5 minutes after removing from oven. Remove from tins and cool on wire racks.

Yield: about ½ dozen

Raisin Bran Muffins

A healthy, high-fiber muffin that's best when served fresh from the oven.

1½ cups miller's bran
1 cup whole wheat pastry flour
1 teaspoon baking soda
¼ teaspoon salt
1 tablespoon granular lecithin

½ cup mild-flavored honey
2 tablespoons vegetable oil
¾ cup orange juice
½ cup raisins
¼ cup chopped walnuts (optional)

● Combine the first five ingredients in a mixing bowl. Add honey, vegetable oil and orange juice. Mix lightly just until blended. ● Stir in raisins and nuts. Fill greased muffin tins ⅔ full. ● Bake at 375° F. for 12 to 15 minutes.

Note: Miller's bran is plain, coarse bran as opposed to bran cereals. It is sold in health food stores and many grocery stores.

Yield: about 1 dozen

Lemon Muffins

Enjoy this crisp and light muffin at breakfast time or for dessert. This recipe adapts beautifully to create many new and tasty variations. Try our five combinations listed below or create your own.

1 cup whole wheat pastry flour	¾ teaspoon grated lemon peel
1 cup unbleached white flour	1 8-ounce carton (1 cup) lemon flavored yogurt
½ cup sugar	
1 tablespoon baking powder	½ cup milk
½ teaspoon baking soda	⅓ cup butter, melted
¼ teaspoon salt	

● Combine dry ingredients. ● Mix together yogurt, milk and melted butter. Add to dry ingredients, stirring just until moistened. Spoon batter into greased 2½-inch muffin tins, filling them ⅔ full. ● Bake at 400° F. for about 20 minutes.

Note: Resist the temptation to fill muffin tins more than ⅔ full. It causes the muffins to rise without side support and they may fall. If some of the pans in your tin are not filled with batter, add two tablespoons of water to each. This protects the pan and provides for more even baking.

Variations:

Honey Granola Muffins: Substitute ⅓ cup honey for sugar. Omit lemon peel. Use vanilla flavored yogurt. Add ½ cup crunchy granola.

Blueberry Muffins: Omit lemon peel. Use vanilla or lemon flavored yogurt. Fold in 1 cup fresh blueberries.

Spiced Apple Muffins: Omit lemon peel and use apple or unflavored yogurt. Add ½ teaspoon ground cinnamon, ¼ teaspoon ground nutmeg, ½ cup chopped pecans and ½ cup finely chopped, pared apple.

Pina Colada Muffins: Omit lemon peel and use pineapple flavored yogurt. Add ¼ teaspoon vanilla extract and ½ cup shredded coconut.

Marmalade Pecan Muffins: Reduce sugar to ¼ cup. Use unflavored yogurt. Add 2 tablespoons marmalade and ½ cup chopped pecans.

Yield: 16 to 18 muffins

Doughnuts

These iced cake doughnuts are delicious served with apple cider or coffee for a special treat.

½	cup butter, at room temperature	2	teaspoons salt
1	cup sugar	2	teaspoons ground nutmeg
1	teaspoon grated lemon peel	1	cup milk
2	teaspoons dry egg replacer		*Glaze:*
¼	cup water	2	cups sifted confectioners' sugar
4½	cups unbleached white flour	1	teaspoon grated lemon peel
2	teaspoons baking powder	3	tablespoons lemon juice or water

● Cream butter, sugar and lemon peel together. Add dry egg replacer and water. Beat well.
● Sift flour with baking powder, salt and nutmeg. Add to the creamed mixture, alternating with milk. Mix just until well blended. (Dough will have the consistency of a heavy cookie batter.) Cover dough and chill for 1 to 2 hours. ● Remove from refrigerator. Place on a lightly floured surface and roll or press to ½-inch thickness. Cut with a floured doughnut cutter. Let stand for 10 to 15 minutes. ● Meanwhile, heat vegetable oil to 370° to 375° F. Carefully lift doughnuts with a spatula and lower into hot oil. Fry 2 or 3 at a time for a few minutes until golden, turning to cook both sides. Drain on paper towels. ● Combine ingredients for glaze. Spread glaze over warm doughnuts.

Yield: 1½ dozen

Oatmeal Sesame Crackers

This sesame cracker is delightfully crunchy. Great for serving with soups or for healthy snacking.

1	cup quick-cooking rolled oats	⅓	cup water
⅔	cup whole wheat pastry flour	¼	cup vegetable oil
⅓	cup wheat germ	1	tablespoon honey or sugar
½	teaspoon seasoned salt (garlic, celery, etc.)	½	cup sesame seeds

● Combine oats, flour, wheat germ and seasoned salt in a mixing bowl. Stir in water, vegetable oil, honey or sugar and sesame seeds. ● Form dough into a ball and divide in half. Roll dough directly onto two greased cookie sheets to form a 12 × 8-inch rectangle on each. Cut into 2-inch squares. ● Bake at 350° F. for about 20 minutes until crisped. Remove from sheets and let cool on wire racks. Store in a tightly sealed container.

Yield: 4 dozen

Rich Croutons

Soup becomes special with the addition of these flavorful, toasted croutons. Good with salads, too.

12 slices of bread	1 teaspoon crumbled dry basil
6 tablespoons butter or 4 tablespoons butter and 2 tablespoons olive oil	1 teaspoon crumbled dry oregano
1 teaspoon garlic salt	2 tablespoons grated Parmesan cheese (optional)

● Cut bread into small cubes and place in a mixing bowl. ● Melt butter and stir in remaining ingredients. Pour over bread and toss to coat. ● Place on an ungreased baking pan with sides. Bake at 375° F. for about 15 minutes until crisped and browned, stirring occasionally. Watch closely to avoid over-toasting, as cooking time depends on crouton size and dryness of the bread.

Note: Freeze leftover croutons in a tightly sealed plastic bag. Thaw at room temperature and heat briefly in a 300° F. oven to re-crisp.

Yield: about 4 cups

Herbed Italian Bread

Your kitchen will be filled with the fragrance of Italian herbs when making this easy oven-browned bread.

1 long loaf Italian or French bread	½ teaspoon crumbled dry basil
½ cup butter, melted	½ teaspoon crumbled dry tarragon
½ cup olive oil	½ teaspoon crumbled dry savory
1 teaspoon onion powder	Pinch of salt or to taste
½ teaspoon crumbled dry oregano	

● Cut bread into 1-inch thick slices. ● Stir together remaining ingredients. Spoon or brush the mixture onto both sides of the bread slices. ● Place in a single layer on an ungreased baking sheet with sides. Bake at 350° F. for 15 minutes or until golden. ● To serve, line a basket with a cloth napkin and pile hot bread inside.

Yield: 8 servings

Sandwiches

Spreads

All-American Tofu Sandwiches

Popular flavors team up with sautéed sliced tofu for these satisfying sandwiches.

1 **pound firm tofu**	**Prepared mustard or ketchup**
2 **tablespoons vegetable oil**	**Eggless Mayonnaise**
1 **tablespoon tamari**	**Sliced tomato**
Garlic powder	**Alfalfa sprouts**
8 **slices whole wheat bread**	

● Cut tofu into wide slices, ½ inch thick. Let drain on paper towels. ● Heat vegetable oil in a large skillet. Fry tofu slices over medium-low heat until browned on both sides. Sprinkle tamari and garlic to taste over slices while frying. Drain on paper towels. ● Assemble sandwiches with remaining ingredients and tofu slices.

Yield: 4 sandwiches

Italian Hero

A chewy hero bread shell is filled with Italian delicacies.

1 **hero bread roll, about 8 inches long**	3 **ounces sliced mozzarella cheese**
½ **cup chopped marinated artichoke hearts and/or marinated mushrooms, drained**	3 **thin slices red onion**
	Sliced tomato

● Make a canoe out of the roll by slicing off a lid about ½ inch from the top. Scoop out the soft bread from the large portion, leaving about ½ inch on all sides. (Inner bread can be saved for bread crumbs.) ● Layer ingredients into bread shell in order given, ending with tomato. Drizzle a little of the artichoke or mushroom marinade over tomato. Top with the bread lid.

Yield: 1 large sandwich

Submarine Sandwich

As much fun to make as it is to eat.

1 **Italian roll**	1 **small tomato, sliced**
Eggless Mayonnaise	1 **cooked vegetarian hot dog, quartered lengthwise**
Prepared mustard	**Sweet pickle chips**
Shredded lettuce	
Sliced cheese	

● Partially slice the roll and open it. Spread Eggless Mayonnaise on one side and mustard on the other. Layer in remaining ingredients.

Yield: 1 large sandwich

Sandwiches

Soy Dogs With Sauerkraut

Here is an old standby with new variations.

1 cup ketchup	Chopped onion
2 tablespoons olive oil	Prepared mustard
1 teaspoon honey	1 cup sauerkraut, well drained
8 vegetarian hot dogs with buns	

● Combine ketchup, olive oil and honey in a saucepan. Add vegetarian hot dogs. Bring to a low boil. Reduce heat and simmer covered for 15 minutes. ● Warm buns in oven at low setting. Remove hot dogs from sauce and place in buns. Spoon some of the sauce over each hot dog. Top with chopped onion, mustard to taste and a row of sauerkraut.

Yield: 8 servings

Vegetarian Reuben Sandwich

Sauerkraut lovers will savor this sandwich which can be served either hot or cold.

2 slices rye bread, lightly toasted	½ cup well drained sauerkraut
Prepared mustard	¼ cup sliced onion, sautéed
Eggless Mayonnaise or butter	Tomato slices
Sliced Swiss cheese	

● Spread bread with mustard and Eggless Mayonnaise or butter. Arrange remaining ingredients on bottom slice and cover with top slice of bread.

Variation: For hot open-faced sandwiches, divide ingredients evenly on two slices of toast. Place on a baking sheet and bake at 400° F. for about 10 minutes.

Yield: 1 serving

Hummus Pita Sandwiches

A very tasty and nutritious sandwich. Serve with Curried Cauliflower Soup for a scrumptious lunch.

2 pita breads	Chopped scallions
1 cup Hummus	Alfalfa sprouts
Cherry tomatoes, halved	Tamari
Chopped bell peppers	

● Cut pita breads in half and open pockets. Place a layer of Hummus spread in the bottom of each pocket. Fill generously with tomatoes, bell peppers, scallions and sprouts. Drizzle a little tamari over the top of the filling.

Yield: 4 pita sandwiches

93

Sloppy Joes

Vegetarian burger, in a bubbling-hot sweet and sour sauce, is spooned over buns for a hearty dish. A favorite with children.

1 large onion, diced	1 tablespoon prepared mustard
½ cup minced celery or green bell pepper	1 tablespoon tamari
3 tablespoons vegetable oil	2 tablespoons vinegar or lemon juice
Dash of garlic powder	1 tablespoon honey or brown sugar
1 16-ounce can vegeburger	Dash of cayenne pepper
1 cup ketchup	Black pepper to taste

● In a large skillet, sauté onion and celery or bell pepper in vegetable oil until onion is soft.
● Add all remaining ingredients. Mix well and bring to a low simmer. Cover and cook over low heat for 10 to 15 minutes, stirring occasionally. Add a small amount of water if needed.
● Serve hot in burger-style buns.

Yield: 4 to 6 servings

Tacos

One of Mexico's most popular dishes. Our version, with well-seasoned beans and a wonderful array of condiments, is fun to assemble and delicious to eat.

12 medium-sized taco shells
Bean Filling:
1 large onion, chopped
2 tablespoons vegetable oil
½ green bell pepper, chopped
2 tablespoons chili powder
1 tablespoon tamari, or salt to taste
3 cups cooked pinto beans, mashed or puréed

Condiments:
Dairy sour cream
Chopped tomatoes
Shredded lettuce
Alfalfa sprouts
Grated cheese
Guacamole
Taco sauce

● Arrange taco shells on a baking pan according to package instructions. Set aside. ● In a large skillet, sauté onion in vegetable oil until softened. Add remaining filling ingredients and cook over low heat for 10 to 15 minutes, stirring frequently. ● Prepare condiments and place in serving bowls. ● Heat taco shells according to package instructions. To serve, place a large spoonful of bean filling in the bottom of each taco shell and let your guests add their own condiments.

Yield: 12 tacos

Tostadas

Crisp corn tortillas, mounded high with delectable toppings.

⅓	cup vegetable oil	
4	medium-sized corn tortillas	
1	cup cooked pinto beans, mashed	
	Chopped tomatoes	
	Sliced black olives	

Chopped scallions
Shredded lettuce
Sliced avocado
Taco sauce

● Heat vegetable oil in a skillet. Fry tortillas in medium-hot oil until lightly crisped. Drain on paper towels. ● Arrange tortillas in a single layer on baking sheets. Spread a layer of mashed beans on each tortilla. Top generously with chopped tomatoes, black olives and scallions. Bake at 350° F. for about 10 minutes until edges of tortillas are well crisped. ● Remove from oven and arrange lettuce and sliced avocados over top. Serve at once with taco sauce.

Yield: 4 servings

Burritos

Soft flour tortillas are wrapped around a savory filling.

3 tablespoons vegetable oil
2 medium-sized scallions, sliced
½ cup chopped green bell peppers
2 garlic cloves, crushed
1 cup tomato sauce
1⅔ cups drained, cooked red kidney
 beans (one 15-ounce can)
 Dash of hot pepper sauce or more
 to taste

1 14-ounce can vegetarian sausage,
 drained and finely chopped
1 fresh tomato, coarsely chopped
2 teaspoons chili powder
2 teaspoons vinegar
½ teaspoon salt
1½ cups shredded jack or Cheddar
 cheese
6 6-inch flour tortillas

● Heat 1 tablespoon of the vegetable oil in a 2-quart saucepan. Stir in scallions and green peppers. Sauté 1 minute. Add 1 crushed garlic clove, stirring briefly. Mix in tomato sauce, beans and hot pepper sauce. Simmer uncovered over medium-low heat for 15 minutes until thickened. ● Meanwhile, heat 2 tablespoons vegetable oil in a skillet. Add chopped vegetarian sausage, fresh tomato, chili powder, vinegar, salt and remaining crushed garlic clove. Cook and stir over medium heat for about 8 minutes. ● Combine bean and vegetarian sausage mixtures. Spread about ½ cup over each tortilla. Sprinkle with cheese. Place under a preheated broiler until cheese melts. Roll and arrange seam side down on a serving plate. May be eaten plain or served topped with sprouts, taco sauce and a spoonful of sour cream or guacamole.

Yield: 6 burritos

Tofu Tortilla Roll-Ups

Tofu adapts beautifully to the flavors of Mexico in this pleasing complete-protein dish.

2   medium-sized onions, chopped
2   medium-sized green bell peppers, chopped
2   tablespoons vegetable oil
1   pound tofu, coarsely mashed and drained
1   tablespoon chili powder or to taste
1   garlic clove, crushed or ¼ teaspoon powder
¾   teaspoon salt or to taste

Freshly ground black pepper
8   5-inch flour tortillas
1   large avocado, cut into 16 slices (optional)
2   cups shredded cheese
Topping:
   Alfalfa sprouts
   Taco sauce
   Dairy sour cream

● Sauté onions and bell peppers in vegetable oil until soft. Add tofu, chili powder, garlic, salt and pepper to taste. Cook over medium-low heat until excess liquid evaporates, stirring occasionally. ● Place tortillas flat on baking sheets. Divide tofu between them, spreading a thin layer over each one. Top each with 2 avocado slices and ¼ cup cheese. ● Place under broiler just until cheese bubbles. Remove and roll up. Place on a serving plate, seam side down. Serve topped with sprouts, taco sauce and sour cream.

Yield: 8 roll-ups

Quick Cheese Enchiladas

A wonderful vegetable and cheese filling is encased in corn tortillas and smothered in traditional enchilada sauce.

½   cup shredded jack cheese
½   cup shredded Cheddar or colby cheese
4   medium-sized scallions, chopped or ½ cup chopped green bell pepper
½   cup chopped fresh mushrooms
½   cup corn kernels, fresh (or frozen and defrosted)
10   5-inch corn tortillas

Sauce:
1½   cups enchilada sauce
   Dash of hot pepper sauce or to taste
½   cup corn kernels, fresh (or frozen and defrosted)
   Chopped chili peppers to taste (optional)
Garnish:
   Sliced black olives

● Mix first 5 ingredients together. ● Arrange tortillas flat on baking sheets. Divide mixture between tortillas, placing about ¼ cup in a single row down the center of each tortilla. Broil under a preheated broiler just until cheese melts. ● Remove from oven and roll tortillas tightly. Place seam side down in an oiled oblong baking pan. Set aside. ● Combine sauce ingredients. Pour evenly over tortillas. Garnish with sliced olives. Bake at 350° F. for 8 to 10 minutes.

Yield: 5 servings

Sandwiches

Asparagus Rarebit

Tender asparagus in a delightful sauce is served over crisp toast for a satisfying hot open-faced sandwich.

12	medium-sized asparagus spears, cut into 1-inch sections, steamed	4	slices of toast
1	cup Cheese Sauce (below)		Paprika

● Drain asparagus well and add to hot Cheese Sauce. ● Place one slice of toast on each

Variation: Use thin broccoli spears or whole asparagus spears. Steam until tender, then drain. Spoon cheese sauce over toast and arrange spears on top of sauce.

Yield: 4 servings

Cheese Sauce

An exceptionally versatile cheese sauce.

3	tablespoons butter	1½	cups milk
3	tablespoons unbleached white or whole wheat flour	1½	teaspoons tamari
1	teaspoon powdered dry mustard	1½	cups shredded Cheddar cheese (8 ounces)
¼	teaspoon salt (optional)		A few drops of hot pepper sauce

● In a medium-sized saucepan, melt butter, then stir in flour, dry mustard and salt. Cook over low heat, stirring constantly, for 1 minute. ● Slowly add milk, stirring briskly to avoid lumps. Add tamari and cook, stirring constantly, until sauce is thickened. ● Stir in shredded cheese and hot pepper sauce. Cook until cheese is melted.

Note: This recipe can be halved for use in recipes requiring 1 cup of Cheese Sauce.

Yield: about 2 cups

Broiled Bean Sandwiches

Follow this recipe for wholesome hot sandwiches that will gratify the most avid appetite. A creative use for leftover beans.

1	cup cooked kidney beans or lentils, well drained and mashed	½	cup chopped onion
2	to 3 tablespoons ketchup	2	ounces Cheddar cheese, sliced or shredded
½	teaspoon curry powder		Alfalfa sprouts
2	whole pita breads		Sliced tomato

● In a small saucepan, heat beans or lentils with ketchup and curry powder. Preheat broiler.
● Spread mixture on top of pita bread. Sprinkle with onion, then top with cheese to cover. Place under broiler until cheese melts. Watch closely. ● Remove to serving plates. Pile alfalfa sprouts on top and decorate with tomato slices. Serve at once.

Yield: 2 open-faced sandwiches

Hot Mushroom Sandwiches

Make these elegant sandwiches for a luncheon or light supper.

4	slices whole wheat bread, freshly toasted	¼	cup sliced scallions
	Blue Cheese Butter	1	small avocado, sliced
	Lettuce leaves	1	tomato, sliced
1	cup sliced fresh mushrooms, sautéed in butter or vegetable oil	½	cup alfalfa sprouts

● Spread the four slices of toast generously with Blue Cheese Butter. ● Layer remaining ingredients on two of the slices. (Mushrooms should be hot.) Top with remaining slices of toast. Serve at once.

Yield: 2 servings

Special Pita Pizza

Pizza prepared west-coast style — casual, quick and nutritious.

1	pita bread	3	tablespoons chopped marinated artichoke hearts
3	tablespoons tomato or marinara sauce	2	tablespoons chopped green bell pepper
	Pinch of crumbled dry basil		Shredded mozzarella or Swiss cheese
	Pinch of crumbled dry oregano	1	teaspoon olive oil
	Dash of garlic powder	1	teaspoon tamari
2	tablespoons sliced scallions		
¼	cup sliced fresh mushrooms		

● Place pita bread on a baking sheet. ● Stir together tomato sauce, basil, oregano and garlic powder. Spread over pita. ● Combine vegetables and cheese in a small bowl. Drizzle olive oil and tamari over top. Toss to mix. Spoon onto pita. ● Bake at 375° F. for about 15 minutes until pita is crisp and cheese is golden.

Yield: 1 serving

Caponata Pita Sandwich

Handy pita pocket bread makes the perfect envelope for this savory Italian filling.

1	pita bread	1	ounce shredded or sliced cheese
½	cup Caponata		

● Slice pita bread in half and open pocket. Fill one half with Caponata and cheese. Wrap in foil and bake at 350° F. until warmed through.

Yield: 1 sandwich

Skillet Cheese Sandwich

A hot and toasty grilled cheese sandwich is always enjoyed. The addition of sliced tomato, onion, vegetarian bacon bits and seasoning makes this version of an American classic especially good. For variety, use different cheeses such as colby, Muenster, Swiss or caraway-jack.

2   slices whole wheat bread, lightly
        buttered on one side
2   ounces sliced cheese
1   thin onion slice

Thin slices of tomato
Vegetarian bacon bits
Garlic powder or curry powder
Black pepper to taste

● Place one slice of bread, buttered side down, in a small skillet. Arrange cheese, onion and tomato on bread. Sprinkle with vegetarian bacon bits and a pinch of garlic powder or curry powder. Add pepper to taste. ● Top with other slice of bread, buttered side up. Place a lid on the skillet and cook over medium-low heat until bottom slice is browned and toasty. Turn with a spatula and brown other side. Cheese should be well melted. Serve at once.

Yield: 1 serving

Quesadillas

Quesadillas are large, crisply fried tortilla turnovers. Our recipe, with its rich cheese filling, makes an impressive brunch when served with browned vegetarian sausages.

3   cups shredded Cheddar cheese
½   cup crumbled firm tofu, drained
½   cup large curd cottage cheese, drained
½   teaspoon turmeric
      Salt and pepper
1   large red bell pepper, sliced
        lengthwise into ¼-inch strips

¼   cup vegetarian bacon bits (optional)
      Chopped chili peppers to
        taste (optional)
¼   cup chopped fresh chives (optional)
5   7-inch flour tortillas
      Butter and vegetable oil for
        skillet-frying

● In a bowl, combine 1 cup of the Cheddar cheese with tofu, cottage cheese, turmeric, and salt and pepper to taste. Mix in bell pepper along with your choice of optional ingredients. ● Warm both sides of tortillas, one at a time, in an ungreased heavy skillet over medium heat. Place on a flat surface. Sprinkle ¼ cup cheese over each tortilla. Spread about ¼ cup of tofu mixture over cheese, leaving a ¼ inch border around edge uncovered. ● Fold tortilla in half, tucking filling in. ● Melt 1 tablespoon butter and 1 tablespoon vegetable oil in a skillet. Fry folded tortillas over medium heat on both sides until crisp. Add more butter and oil as needed. ● Keep Quesadillas warm in oven until served. Sprinkle remaining cheese over top just before serving.

Variation: Spoon heated chili over top of fried Quesadillas before sprinkling with cheese.

Yield: 5 servings

Hot Curry & Cheese Muffins

Appetizing hot open-faced sandwiches, superb for luncheon fare or hors d'oeuvres.

6	medium-sized scallions, thinly sliced	2	teaspoons curry powder or to taste
1½	cups shredded sharp Cheddar cheese	1	cup chopped black olives
½	cup Eggless Mayonnaise	6	English muffins, halved and toasted

● Combine first five ingredients. Spread generously on toasted muffin halves. ● Place under a preheated broiler just until cheese melts. Watch closely.

Note: For quick appetizers, slice each muffin half into wedges before broiling.

Yield: 12 muffins

Hot Cinnamon Nut Sandwiches

These enjoyable sandwiches are welcome at breakfast or lunch.

¼	cup peanut butter	4	slices whole grain bread, freshly toasted
2	teaspoons honey		
¼	teaspoon ground cinnamon	4	ounces Cheddar cheese, sliced or shredded
1	large apple, thinly sliced		
1	teaspoon lemon juice		

● Stir together peanut butter, honey and cinnamon. ● Toss apple with lemon juice to prevent discoloration. ● Spread peanut butter mixture on 4 slices of toast. Cover with apple slices, then cheese. ● Place open-faced sandwiches on a baking sheet. Broil under a preheated broiler until cheese melts. Watch closely.

Yield: 4 open-faced sandwiches

Peanut Butter Special

For a departure from the ordinary, try this tasty combination.

2	slices wheat toast		Cucumber slices
1	tablespoon peanut butter	1	ounce cheese slice
	Tomato slices		Dash of tamari
	Lettuce		

● Spread peanut butter on both slices of toast. Layer tomato, lettuce, cucumber and cheese on one slice. Drizzle a little tamari over filling. Top with other slice.

Yield: 1 sandwich

Red & White Tea Sandwiches

Serve these charming little sandwiches at an afternoon tea party.

1 8-ounce package cream cheese, at room temperature	½ cup shredded coconut
10 thin slices of wheat or pumpernickel bread	½ cup finely chopped pecans or walnuts
	20 small fresh strawberries, stemmed and halved

● Spread cream cheese on bread. Sprinkle with coconut and nuts. ● Cut each slice into 4 triangles or squares. Garnish each tea sandwich with a halved strawberry.

Yield: 40 tea sandwiches

Banana Cheesecake Sandwich

A fragrant combination of flavors that is absolutely delicious.

¼ cup ricotta cheese	⅛ teaspoon lemon juice
¼ teaspoon sugar or honey	2 slices banana bread
Pinch of ground cinnamon	Sliced fresh strawberries

● Combine ricotta cheese, sugar or honey, cinnamon and lemon juice. ● Spread on both slices of banana bread. Top one slice with strawberries. Cover with remaining slice.

Yield: 1 sandwich

Triple Decker Sandwich

Impress your guests with this attractive layered loaf. Ideal for picnics or parties.

1 8-inch round Italian bread loaf	*Mexican Filling:*
Mid-Eastern Filling:	Guacamole
Hummus	Deviled Cheese Spread
Tabbouli Salad	Refried pinto beans
Eggplant Caviar	

● Cut bread horizontally three times, into four slices of bread approximately ½ inch thick depending on size of loaf. Use a long serrated knife for best results. ● Spread a generous amount of Hummus or Guacamole mixture on bottom slice, then cover with next slice of bread. Spread with Tabbouli Salad or Deviled Cheese Spread and cover with next slice. Spread with remaining filling. Top with last crusty slice. ● Wrap loaf firmly in plastic wrap. Refrigerate for 1 hour until set. Remove and slice into wedges. Arrange on a serving plate. Cover with plastic wrap to prevent drying out, and let stand ½ hour to take the chill off before serving.

Yield: 6 to 8 servings

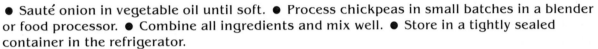

Chickpea Artichoke Spread

A marvelous combination of flavors and textures makes this spread outstanding.

1	medium-sized onion, chopped	1	tablespoon lemon juice
1	tablespoon vegetable oil	½	cup Eggless Mayonnaise
1	15-ounce can chickpeas, drained	½	teaspoon onion powder
1	cup finely chopped canned or marinated artichoke hearts, drained	1	cup chopped celery (optional)

● Sauté onion in vegetable oil until soft. ● Process chickpeas in small batches in a blender or food processor. ● Combine all ingredients and mix well. ● Store in a tightly sealed container in the refrigerator.

Yield: 2 cups

Hummus

Here is an adaptation of one of the most well-known Middle-Eastern dishes. The blend of seasonings in this spread makes a very special pita sandwich when stuffed with an assortment of fresh vegetables and sprinkled with tamari.

2	cups cooked chickpeas	2	tablespoons tamari
⅓	cup tahini	1	teaspoon crumbled dry basil
¼	cup dairy sour cream	1	teaspoon dried rosemary
2	tablespoons lemon juice	½	teaspoon crumbled dry thyme
2	tablespoons olive oil	½	teaspoon rubbed sage

● Process chickpeas in small batches in a blender or food processor. Combine with remaining ingredients.

Yield: 2½ cups

Yellow Split Pea Spread

This enjoyable filling, with its perky flavor of ginger, makes a distinctive sandwich spread.

1 cup cooked yellow split peas (very thick)	½ teaspoon turmeric
	Dash of cayenne pepper
2 tablespoons butter, at room temperature	½ cup cottage cheese
	¼ cup chopped celery
½ teaspoon salt	¼ cup chopped onion (optional)
¼ teaspoon powdered ginger	

● Stir together cooked split peas, butter, salt, ginger, turmeric and cayenne. Add remaining ingredients. ● Chill before using.

Note: This is a handy use for leftover split peas. To start from scratch, simmer ½ cup dried split peas uncovered in 1½ cups water until soft and thick.

Yield: 2 cups

Cottage Cheese & Olive Spread

Tamari, chili sauce and ripe olives add a special touch to this cottage cheese recipe.

1 cup cottage cheese	½ cup chopped ripe olives
½ teaspoon tamari	Salt and pepper to taste
2 tablespoons chili sauce	

● Process cottage cheese in blender until smooth. Stir in remaining ingredients. ● Store in a tightly sealed container in the refrigerator.

Yield: 1½ cups

Sandwiches

Sesame & Green Pea Spread

*Green peas and roasted sesame seeds make this a nice change-of-pace sandwich spread.
Serve on rounds of rye crisps or wheat crackers for an excellent appetizer.*

¼ cup hulled sesame seeds	¼ cup water
2 tablespoons butter	1 teaspoon tamari
1 small onion, chopped	½ teaspoon salt
1 garlic clove, minced	2 teaspoons lemon juice
1 10-ounce package frozen peas	

● Toast sesame seeds in a heavy ungreased skillet over medium heat until lightly browned.
Remove and set aside. ● Melt butter in the same skillet. Add onion and garlic and sauté until
onion is soft. Stir in frozen peas, ¼ cup water, tamari and salt. Cook about 5 minutes until
peas are just tender. ● Purée pea mixture in a blender with lemon juice. Remove to a bowl
and stir in sesame seeds. ● Store in a covered container in the refrigerator.

Yield: about 2 cups

Almond Mushroom Spread

*Crunchy bits of almonds in a pâté of mushrooms, onions and garlic make this perfect for
sandwiches or canapés.*

1 cup slivered almonds	½ teaspoon salt
¼ cup butter	¼ teaspoon ground thyme
1 small onion, chopped	⅛ teaspoon black pepper
¾ pound fresh mushrooms, sliced	2 tablespoons vegetable oil
1 garlic clove, minced	

● Toast almonds in a heavy ungreased skillet over low heat for about 5 minutes. Remove and
set aside. ● Melt butter in the same skillet. Add onion and sauté 5 minutes. Stir in
mushrooms, garlic, salt, thyme and black pepper. Cook over low heat, stirring frequently,
until liquid evaporates. ● Reserve 2 tablespoons of the toasted almonds. Place remaining
almonds in blender with mushroom mixture. Add vegetable oil and process until puréed.
Remove from blender to a bowl. Stir in reserved almonds. Store in a covered container in the
refrigerator.

Yield: 1½ cups

Peanut Sesame Spread

Peanut butter gets a special boost in flavor and nutrition in this popular spread. Children love it.

1	cup peanut butter	½	cup honey
1	cup sesame butter	½	cup chopped sunflower seeds

● Mix well and refrigerate.

Yield: 3 cups

Apple Peanut Butter Spread

Lots of crunchy shredded apple adds texture to this easy spread.

⅔	cup shredded or finely chopped apple	1½	tablespoons peanut butter
1	teaspoon lemon juice		Eggless Mayonnaise

● In a small bowl, toss apple with lemon juice. Stir in peanut butter and enough Eggless Mayonnaise to make a good spreading consistency.

Yield: about ⅔ cup

Indonesian Peanut Spread

An Indonesian spread that combines peanut butter, flaked coconut and zesty red chili peppers in a festive way.

1	medium-sized onion, chopped	½	teaspoon salt
1	garlic clove, minced	⅔	cup peanut butter
1½	teaspoons peanut or vegetable oil	2	tablespoons water
½	cup flaked coconut	¼	to ½ teaspoon finely chopped dried red chili pepper
1	teaspoon grated lemon rind	⅛	teaspoon grated fresh ginger

● Sauté onion and garlic in vegetable oil until soft. Combine with remaining ingredients.

Yield: about 2½ cups

Tofu Miso Spread

A good high-protein spread.

1   cup soft tofu, drained
1   tablespoon natto or barley miso

2   tablespoons nutritional yeast
2   scallions, finely chopped

● Mash all ingredients together. Refrigerate until ready to serve.

Yield: 1½ cups

Herb & Avocado Spread

For a quick and pleasing sandwich, start with your favorite bread, pita or bagel, then layer with cream cheese, Herb & Avocado Spread, alfalfa sprouts and sliced tomatoes.

1   small avocado, mashed
1   teaspoon lemon juice
½   garlic clove, minced
1   tablespoon minced scallions

1   tablespoon chopped fresh parsley
    Pinch of chili powder
    Salt to taste

● Combine all ingredients. Refrigerate and use within 8 hours.

Yield: ⅔ cup

Avocado & Cheese Spread

Cheese, avocado and the distinctive flavor of tamari make this one of our most pleasing spreads.

1   small avocado, mashed
½   teaspoon fresh lime juice
¼   cup shredded Cheddar or jack cheese
1   tablespoon chopped fresh parsley

1   tablespoon dairy sour cream
½   teaspoon tamari
1   tablespoon chopped chives or
    scallions

● Combine all ingredients. Refrigerate and use within 8 hours.

Yield: ⅔ cup

Zippy Avocado Spread

Horseradish adds the zip here.

½ cup mashed avocado
1 teaspoon tamari
2 teaspoons fresh lemon juice

½ teaspoon prepared horseradish
¼ teaspoon garlic salt

● Combine all ingredients. Refrigerate and use within 8 hours.

Yield: ½ cup

Cream Cheese Honey Spread

This easy spread is especially nice on our Quick Cinnamon Raisin Bread.

1 3-ounce package cream cheese, at
   room temperature

¼ cup honey
¼ cup ground pecans, walnuts or almonds

● Combine all ingredients. Store in a tightly sealed container in the refrigerator.

Yield: 1 cup

Orange Cream Cheese Spread

Colorful and refreshing, this makes an attractive spread for canapé sandwiches or toast.

1 8-ounce package cream cheese, at
   room temperature
1¼ teaspoons grated orange rind

1 medium orange, peeled, sectioned
   and chopped
1 tablespoon mild honey

● Combine all ingredients. ● Store in a tightly sealed container in the refrigerator.

Yield: about 1¾ cups

Liptauer Cheese

This classic German cheese spread is full of flavor and improves with a few days of ripening.

¼ cup butter, at room temperature
2½ tablespoons vegetable oil
1 cup cream cheese or cottage cheese,
 at room temperature
1 to 2 teaspoons chopped capers
⅓ cup minced fresh onion

1 tablespoon caraway seeds, ground
⅛ teaspoon black pepper
1 garlic clove, minced
⅛ teaspoon cayenne pepper
½ teaspoon salt or to taste
2 to 3 teaspoons prepared mustard

● Cream together butter and vegetable oil. Stir in cream cheese or cottage cheese. Add all other ingredients and mix with a fork or beat until smooth. ● For best flavor, refrigerate in a tightly sealed container for 3 days before using.

Yield: 1½ cups

Cheese Slaw Spread

Colorful fresh vegetables and shredded cheese are the main ingredients in this handy sandwich filling.

1 cup shredded carrots
1 green bell pepper, diced
1 cup shredded red cabbage
1¼ cups shredded Cheddar cheese

¼ cup finely chopped onion
¼ cup Eggless Mayonnaise
1 teaspoon prepared mustard
2 tablespoons ketchup

● Mix all ingredients together. Chill in refrigerator before using as a sandwich filling or salad.

Yield: 2 cups

Deviled Cheese Spread

Use extra-sharp Cheddar cheese for even more flavor in this tangy spread.

1 cup shredded Cheddar or jack cheese
¼ teaspoon salt
1 teaspoon paprika
½ teaspoon tamari

½ teaspoon vinegar
½ teaspoon prepared mustard
 Pinch of cayenne pepper
1 teaspoon peanut or sesame butter

● Combine all ingredients, mixing thoroughly. ● Store in a tightly sealed container in refrigerator.

Yield: 1 cup   109

Pimento Cheese Spread

A versatile mixture to keep on hand for sandwiches. Also makes a wonderful snack when stuffed in celery.

½   pound sharp Cheddar cheese,
        shredded and at room temperature
¼   cup finely chopped pimento

Eggless Mayonnaise
Dash of black pepper

● Combine all ingredients, using enough Eggless Mayonnaise for a smooth-spreading consistency. Chill before using.

Yield: about 2 cups

Eastern Tofu Spread

Crunchy vegetables add texture to this nourishing spread.

8   ounces firm tofu, drained
¼   cup chopped green or red bell pepper
2   scallions, sliced
¼   cup shredded carrots
2   tablespoons chopped fresh parsley
¼   cup tahini, at room temperature

¼   teaspoon garlic powder
2   teaspoons lemon juice
1   teaspoon tamari
¼   teaspoon salt
½   teaspoon ground cumin

● Mash tofu in a bowl. Add all other ingredients and mix well.

Yield: 2 cups

Seasoned Butters

These simple butters will add flavor and flair to your sandwiches, canapés or cooked vegetables. Combine softened butter with seasonings and store in tightly sealed containers in the refrigerator.

Chili Butter: 3 tablespoons chili sauce, ⅛ teaspoon lemon juice, ½ cup butter

Chive Butter: 2 tablespoons minced fresh chives, ½ cup butter

Lemon or Orange Butter: 1 teaspoon lemon or orange juice, ¼ teaspoon grated lemon or orange rind, ½ cup butter

Pecan Butter: 2 tablespoons ground pecans, ¼ teaspoon grated orange rind, ½ cup butter

Parsley Butter: 2 tablespoons finely minced fresh parsley, dash of tamari, ½ cup butter

Blue Cheese Butter: 2 tablespoons blue cheese, dash of tamari, ½ cup butter

Tarragon Butter: 2 finely chopped fresh tarragon leaves, a few drops of vinegar, 1 tablespoon minced pimento, ½ cup butter

Parmesan Butter: 1 tablespoon grated Parmesan cheese, 1½ teaspoons crumbled dry basil, 1 teaspoon crumbled dry marjoram, ½ cup butter

Ginger & Lime Butter: 1 teaspoon grated fresh ginger, ¼ teaspoon black pepper, ½ teaspoon grated lime peel, 2 tablespoons lime juice, ½ cup butter

Burgers

Sauces

Bean & Grain Burgers

Try this adaptation of the Mid-Eastern falafel for a satisfying and complete-protein meal.

1 medium-sized onion, finely chopped	1 cup cooked rice
2 tablespoons vegetable oil	Vegetable oil
2 cups cooked chickpeas, drained	*Garnish:*
1 cup fine fresh bread crumbs	2½ cups alfalfa sprouts
¼ cup tahini	1 cup shredded carrot
¼ cup tamari	2 medium-sized tomatoes, cut into
2 large garlic cloves, crushed or	thin wedges
½ teaspoon powder	Sesame Tahini Sauce (below)
¼ cup chopped fresh parsley	

● Sauté onion in 2 tablespoons vegetable oil until soft. ● Coarsely mash chickpeas with a potato masher or process lightly in a food processor. Add bread crumbs, tahini, tamari and garlic. Mix thoroughly. ● Stir in sautéed onion, parsley and cooked rice. ● Form into 8 burgers. Skillet-fry in vegetable oil until browned on both sides. ● Serve hot with alfalfa sprouts, shredded carrot and tomato wedges. Spoon Sesame Tahini Sauce over top.

Note: Mixture can also be formed into 1-inch balls and skillet-fried or deep-fried. This size is ideal for use in pita breads.

Yield: 8 burgers

Sesame Tahini Sauce

This sauce will give a special boost to your burgers, salads and grain dishes.

¼ cup light sesame oil	2 tablespoons chopped fresh parsley
¼ cup tahini	¼ cup diced red bell pepper
2 tablespoons tamari	1½ tablespoons unflavored yogurt
2 tablespoons lemon juice	1 teaspoon honey
2 garlic cloves, crushed	

● Combine all ingredients, mixing thoroughly.

Yield: about 1 cup

Lentil Burgers

Walnuts and herbs lend a unique flavor to lentils and brown rice in this hearty burger. Delicious served with melted cheese and Burger Relish on a whole wheat bun.

¾	cup uncooked lentils, rinsed	¼	cup chopped fresh parsley
2	cups water	⅛	teaspoon black pepper
½	teaspoon salt	¼	teaspoon crumbled dry oregano
¼	cup uncooked brown rice	¼	teaspoon crumbled dry basil
1	cup fresh bread crumbs	¼	cup wheat germ, fine dry bread crumbs,
½	cup chopped walnuts		or cracker meal for coating
⅓	cup chopped onion		Vegetable oil
¼	cup chili sauce		

● Combine lentils, water and salt in a 2-quart saucepan. Bring to a boil, then stir in rice. Reduce heat and simmer covered for 45 minutes or until soft. ● Whirl bread crumbs and walnuts together in a food processor, or finely chop walnuts by hand. Combine with bread crumbs in a mixing bowl. Add onion, chili sauce, parsley, pepper, oregano and basil. ● Mash lentils and rice together. Add to bowl and mix thoroughly. Let cool for easy handling. ● Form into 6 burgers. Coat both sides with wheat germ, dry bread crumbs or cracker meal. Skillet-fry in hot vegetable oil until browned on both sides. Serve with ketchup or Burger Relish (below).

Yield: 6 burgers

Burger Relish

Add zip to your burgers with this wonderful tomato relish.

1	medium-sized onion, chopped	2	tablespoons vegetable oil
½	medium-sized red or green bell pepper, chopped	½	cup ketchup
1	stalk celery, chopped	1	tablespoon sweet or India relish
			Dash of hot pepper sauce (optional)

● Sauté onion, bell pepper and celery in vegetable oil until onion is soft. Remove from heat. Stir in ketchup and relish. Add hot pepper sauce if desired. Store in a covered container in refrigerator.

Yield: 1½ cups

Soy Burgers

These classic burgers are noted for their high nutritional value and superb nutty flavor. Try them topped with melted Cheddar cheese and ketchup.

1   medium-sized onion, diced
1   tablespoon vegetable oil
1   15-ounce can soybeans, drained
    (1⅔ cups)
2   garlic cloves, minced
½   cup ketchup

¼   to ½ cup toasted wheat germ
    Salt to taste
1   tablespoon nutritional yeast (optional)
6   ounces cheese, sliced or
    shredded (optional)

● Sauté onion in 1 tablespoon vegetable oil until soft. ● Meanwhile, mash soybeans coarsely in a large bowl. Add garlic, ketchup, wheat germ, salt and nutritional yeast. Stir in sautéed onion. ● Form into 6 burgers. Place on an oiled baking sheet and brush tops of burgers with vegetable oil. Place under a preheated broiler for 5 minutes. Turn with a spatula and broil other side for about 5 more minutes or until browned and crisped. Watch closely. Top with cheese if desired and broil until cheese melts. Serve with ketchup.

Note: These burgers can also be skillet-fried or baked in the oven.

Yield: 6 burgers

Oat Burgers

One of our most popular burgers. Marvelous, not just for their taste, but for ease of preparation as well.

4½   cups water
⅓   cup vegetable oil
⅓   cup tamari
1   large onion, diced
1½   cups chopped fresh mushrooms

1   teaspoon garlic powder
½   teaspoon crumbled dry basil
½   teaspoon crumbled dry oregano
¼   cup nutritional yeast
4½   cups old-fashioned rolled oats

● In a large pot, combine all ingredients except oats and bring to a boil. Reduce heat and stir in oats. Let simmer uncovered for 5 minutes. ● Remove from heat and let stand 1 hour to cool and thicken. ● Form into 16 balls (mixture will be sticky). Place on well-oiled baking sheets and gently press balls to form into patties. ● Bake at 350° F. for 25 minutes. Turn with a spatula and bake 20 more minutes. ● Serve with gravy or Burger Relish.

Note: To freeze, let fried burgers cool, then seal between sheets of plastic wrap or waxed paper.

Yield: 16 burgers

Millet Peanut Burgers

These distinctive millet burgers, rich with seeds and nuts, make a great change-of-pace meal.

½ cup raw sunflower seeds	⅓ cup thick peanut butter
½ cup raw sesame seeds	½ teaspoon salt (optional)
1 cup cooked millet	⅛ teaspoon black pepper
1 cup shredded mild Cheddar or jack cheese	¼ cup warm water
	Vegetable oil

● Process sunflower seeds and sesame seeds together in a blender or food processor until finely chopped. Combine with all other burger ingredients. ● Form into six 4-inch burgers. Skillet-fry in vegetable oil over medium heat until golden brown on both sides. ● Serve with Muenster Sauce (below) or on a bun with relish and a slice of cheese.

Yield: 6 servings

Muenster Sauce

The wonderful flavors of tamari and paprika in this smooth cheese sauce will enhance your burgers, cooked vegetables and grain dishes.

¾ cup water	½ teaspoon paprika
2 tablespoons cornstarch or arrowroot	1 cup diced Muenster cheese
1 to 2 teaspoons tamari	

● Stir water, cornstarch or arrowroot, tamari and paprika together in a small saucepan. Cook uncovered over medium heat for about 5 minutes, stirring constantly, until thickened. ● Add cheese to saucepan. Cook and stir until cheese is melted.

Variation: Use Cheddar cheese instead of Muenster.

Yield: 1 ¾ cups

Rice & Tahini Burgers

These appealing burgers are enriched with miso and tahini for a well-seasoned meal.

1	cup cooked brown rice	1	to 2 tablespoons miso
1	cup ground almonds	3	tablespoons wheat germ
1	cup shredded Swiss cheese	¼	cup water
⅓	cup tahini		Vegetable oil

● Mix all ingredients together, using miso to taste. Form into 6 burgers. ● Skillet-fry in vegetable oil until browned on both sides; or, lightly oil both sides of burgers and place on an oiled baking sheet. Bake at 350° F. for 15 minutes, turn with a spatula, and bake 15 more minutes until browned. ● Serve with Miso Tahini Sauce (below).

Yield: 6 burgers

Miso Tahini Sauce

Here is a full-flavored and nourishing sauce that is excellent when served over burgers, cooked vegetables or grain dishes.

1	small onion, chopped	2	to 4 tablespoons miso
2	tablespoons vegetable oil	¾	to 1½ cups boiling water
¾	cup tahini		

● Sauté onion in vegetable oil until lightly browned. ● Add tahini. Cook and stir for a few minutes until tahini gives off a roasted aroma. ● Remove from heat. Stir in miso to taste. Add ¾ cups water and mix well. Add additional water as needed to make a smooth sauce.

Yield: 2 to 3 cups

Indian Pea Cutlets

We offer our Westernized version of this delicious Indian classic.

1   medium-sized onion, chopped
2   tablespoons butter
1   10-ounce package frozen green
        peas, thawed
1   cup ricotta cheese
1¼ cups (packed) fresh bread crumbs
1   tablespoon lemon juice
¼   cup chopped fresh parsley
1   teaspoon salt

¼   teaspoon cayenne pepper or ½ teaspoon
        chili powder
     Vegetable oil
Coating:
⅓   cup chickpea flour or whole
        wheat flour
     Water
¾   cup fine dry bread crumbs

● In a large skillet, sauté onion in butter for 3 to 5 minutes. Add peas and cook 2 minutes. Remove from heat. Stir in ricotta cheese, fresh bread crumbs, lemon juice, parsley, salt and cayenne pepper or chili powder. Let cool. ● Form into 7 cutlets. Refrigerate at least 30 minutes to firm cutlets for easy handling. ● Gradually add a small amount of water to chickpea or wheat flour to make a mixture the consistency of pancake batter. Dip cutlets into batter, then coat with bread crumbs. ● Skillet-fry in medium-hot vegetable oil until browned on both sides. Serve with chutney or ketchup.

Yield: 7 cutlets

Potato Patties

Hearty golden potato patties, delicately seasoned with curry.

4   raw medium-sized potatoes (about
        1½ pounds), grated
1   medium-sized onion, chopped
1   teaspoon salt
¼   teaspoon black pepper
1   teaspoon curry powder

½   cup frozen or cooked fresh
        peas (optional)
2   tablespoons chopped fresh parsley
¾   cup crumbled firm tofu, drained
½   cup whole wheat flour
     Vegetable oil

● Combine potatoes, onion, seasonings, peas and parsley in a bowl. Add tofu and flour. Use a little additional flour if necessary so patties will hold their shape. ● Form into 8 to 10 patties. Place on generously oiled baking sheets and bake at 375° F. for 15 minutes. Turn with a spatula and bake an additional 15 minutes or until nicely browned. Drain briefly on paper towels.

Yield: 8 to 10 patties

Vegetable Potato Cutlets

Tarragon gives these potato cutlets a gourmet touch. An ideal use for leftover vegetables.

1 10-ounce package frozen mixed vegetables, or 1½ cups leftover cooked vegetables
3 tablespoons butter
1 large onion, chopped
⅔ cup chopped fresh mushrooms
1 large potato, boiled and mashed (1 cup packed)

1 teaspoon (scant) crumbled dry tarragon
½ cup or more fine dry bread crumbs
   Salt and black pepper
   Garlic powder
   Vegetable oil

● Cook frozen vegetables according to package instructions. Drain and set aside to cool.
● Melt butter in a skillet. Sauté onion for 5 minutes. Add mushrooms and sauté until onion is golden. ● Meanwhile, finely chop cooked frozen vegetables or leftovers. ● Combine all cutlet ingredients, seasoning with salt, pepper and garlic to taste. Use enough bread crumbs so that the mixture holds its shape. Form into 6 cutlets. ● Skillet-fry in medium-hot vegetable oil until browned on both sides; or, bake on a greased baking sheet at 375° F. for 15 minutes, turn cutlets with a spatula and bake another 15 minutes until crisped. Serve plain or with Mushroom Gravy (below).

Yield: 6 cutlets

Mushroom Gravy

Lots of sautéed fresh mushrooms lend flavor to this creamy sauce.

1 cup sliced fresh mushrooms
1 tablespoon minced fresh onion
2 tablespoons butter
1½ to 2 tablespoons unbleached white flour

1 cup milk
2 teaspoons tamari
   Black pepper to taste
   Dash of garlic powder

● In a large skillet, sauté mushrooms and onion in butter until soft. Sprinkle flour into skillet and cook, stirring constantly, for 2 minutes. ● Gradually add milk, stirring briskly. Cook and stir over low heat until thickened. Season with tamari, black pepper and garlic powder.

Yield: 2 cups

Sea Cutlets

The interesting flavor of dulse adds a hint of the sea to these chickpea and tofu cutlets. Perfect with our Tartar Sauce.

1⅔ cups cooked chickpeas
2 tablespoons chopped dulse leaves
2 tablespoons finely chopped onion
2 tablespoons finely chopped fresh parsley
¼ cup lemon juice

1 teaspoon tamari
⅛ teaspoon black pepper
¾ cup mashed firm tofu, well drained
1 cup uncooked cornmeal
Vegetable oil

● Coarsely mash chickpeas in a food processor or by hand. Place in a large mixing bowl.
● Soak a few dulse leaves in warm water until softened. Rinse, removing any foreign matter. Chop dulse and measure out 2 tablespoons. Add to chickpeas along with onion, parsley, lemon juice, tamari and black pepper. Stir in tofu and cornmeal. ● Form into 8 cutlets. Skillet-fry in vegetable oil over medium heat for 5 to 10 minutes on each side until nicely browned. ● Serve with Tartar Sauce (below).

Note: Also good as a sandwich with Tartar Sauce, tomatoes and lettuce.

Yield: 8 cutlets

Tartar Sauce

Tangy tartar sauce is traditionally used to enhance deep-fried foods.

½ cup Eggless Mayonnaise
½ cup sweet pickle relish

1 tablespoon minced fresh onion
1 tablespoon capers (optional)

● Stir all ingredients together. Store in a covered container in the refrigerator.

Yield: 1 cup

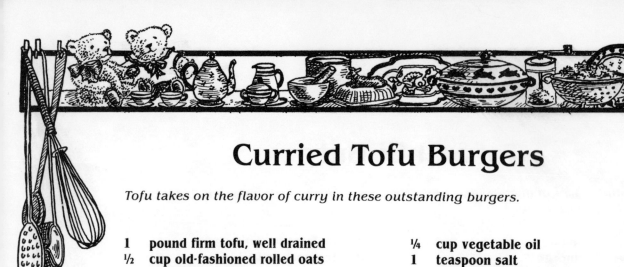

Curried Tofu Burgers

Tofu takes on the flavor of curry in these outstanding burgers.

1 pound firm tofu, well drained	¼ cup vegetable oil
½ cup old-fashioned rolled oats	1 teaspoon salt
1 tablespoon tamari	¼ teaspoon black pepper
2 teaspoons curry powder	Fine dry bread crumbs, wheat germ,
2 tablespoons ketchup	or cornmeal for coating
4 tablespoons raw sunflower seeds	Vegetable oil
¼ cup shredded carrot (optional)	

● Crumble drained tofu into a mixing bowl. ● Process oats in a blender to make a coarse flour. Add to tofu. ● Stir in remaining ingredients except for coating crumbs and vegetable oil. ● Form into 8 burgers. Coat both sides of burgers in crumbs. Skillet-fry in medium-hot vegetable oil until browned on both sides. Or, bake on a greased baking sheet at 375° F. for 15 to 20 minutes. Turn with a spatula and bake another 15 to 20 minutes. Serve with Curried Vegetable Sauce (below).

Yield: 8 burgers

Curried Vegetable Sauce

Laden with an abundance of vegetables, this aromatic sauce is an ideal topping for Curried Tofu Burgers, baked potatoes or grain dishes.

¼ cup peas, fresh or frozen	¼ cup unbleached white flour
¼ cup corn kernels, fresh or frozen	1 teaspoon salt
¼ cup chopped onion	Black pepper to taste
¼ cup chopped red or green bell pepper	½ to 1 teaspoon curry powder
¼ cup shredded carrot	2 or more cups milk
¼ cup butter	½ cup shredded cheese

● Cook fresh peas and corn separately in a small amount of water until tender, or defrost frozen peas and corn. Drain. ● Sauté onion, bell pepper and carrot in butter until soft. Mix in flour, salt, pepper and curry powder, stirring constantly. ● Add 2 cups milk, corn and peas. Cook and stir for 1 to 2 minutes until thick and bubbly. Add cheese and stir until melted. Use additional milk, if needed, for desired consistency.

Yield: about 4 cups

Tofu Chili Burgers

Crunchy corn chips and chili powder add a Mexican accent to these delicious burgers.

1   medium-sized onion, chopped
1   stalk celery, chopped
½   medium-sized green or red bell
     pepper, chopped
2   tablespoons vegetable oil
1   pound firm tofu, drained
1   cup old-fashioned rolled oats
¼   cup vegetable oil
1½ tablespoons ketchup

1   tablespoon chili powder
1   teaspoon salt
¼   teaspoon black pepper or cayenne
     pepper to taste
     Chopped green chili peppers to taste
     Finely crushed taco-flavored corn chips
      for coating
     Vegetable oil for frying

● Sauté onion, celery and bell pepper in 2 tablespoons vegetable oil until soft. ● Crumble tofu into a mixing bowl. Process oats in a blender until the consistency of coarse flour. Add to tofu. Mix in ¼ cup vegetable oil. ● Add sautéed vegetables and ketchup, seasonings and chili peppers. Form into 8 balls. (Moisten hands if necessary — mixture is sticky.) Roll in corn chip crumbs, coating generously. Gently press ball into a flat burger shape. ● Skillet-fry in medium-hot vegetable oil until browned on both sides; or, place on greased baking sheets and bake at 375° F. for 15 minutes, then turn with a spatula and bake 15 more minutes until browned.

Yield: 8 burgers

Bountiful Burgers

A light, crispy coating on the outside with a protein-packed meal on the inside.

3   tablespoons raw sunflower seeds
1   cup rolled oats, instant or
     old-fashioned
2   cups (1 pound) mashed firm tofu,
     well drained
2   cups alfalfa sprouts
2   tablespoons tamari
¼   teaspoon black pepper

½   cup chopped scallions or onion
Coating:
¼   cup nutritional yeast
¼   cup wheat germ
¼   cup cornmeal
¼   teaspoon salt
Also:
     Vegetable oil

● Grind sunflower seeds and oats together in a blender until oats are like a coarse flour. Combine with all remaining burger ingredients. Knead mixture until well mixed. ● Shape into ten 3-inch patties. ● Combine coating ingredients in a wide bowl. Generously coat both sides of burgers. Skillet-fry in ⅛ inch of medium-hot vegetable oil for 3 to 5 minutes on each side until well browned and crisped. ● Serve hot with ketchup or tamari or use in a pita sandwich.

Yield: 10 burgers

Eggless Creations

About Soufflés & Quiches:

Quiches and soufflés are elegant and impressive presentations, yet remarkably simple to prepare. Our quiche recipes start with a flaky pie crust, layers of nicely seasoned vegetables covered with grated cheese and piled high with a ricotta custard that is baked to a golden brown. We have included four exciting versions of this French classic.

Cheese Soufflé

This unique adaptation of the perennial French classic introduces the pleasing flavors of rye, mushrooms and red onion baked in a delectable creamy custard.

3	cups shredded Cheddar cheese	**Custard:**	
6	slices standard-sized rye bread	2	cups milk
1	cup sliced fresh mushrooms	1	pound firm tofu, drained
1	large red onion, chopped	1	teaspoon ground turmeric
1	tablespoon butter	1	teaspoon salt

● Spread 1½ cups of the cheese in the bottom of an oiled deep 2-quart soufflé or straight-sided casserole dish. Arrange the bread slices overlapping each other to completely cover the cheese. Sprinkle remaining cheese over bread. ● Briefly sauté mushrooms and red onion in butter until onion is just softened. Spread over cheese in the dish. ● Whirl custard ingredients together in a blender or food processor. Pour over mushrooms and onion. Let stand at least 30 minutes. (Soufflé may be refrigerated up to several hours at this point. If refrigerated, allow soufflé time to reach room temperature before baking.) ● Place a pan filled with 1 inch of water on an oven rack below the soufflé. Bake soufflé uncovered at 350°F. for 1 hour and 15 minutes or until a knife inserted in the center comes out without custard sticking to it. Serve at once for best appearance.

Note: The soufflé recipe can be used as a base for many variations. Sautéed vegetables can be arranged on the top of the custard before baking (see Quiche recipes in this chapter for ideas) and the types of bread and cheese used can be varied.

Variation: For a quiche-like result, bake in two 9-inch cake pans and reduce baking time. For a single 10-inch quiche pan, use 2 cups shredded Cheddar cheese, 5 slices standard-sized rye bread, ¾ cup sliced fresh mushrooms, 1 medium-sized red onion, 1 tablespoon butter. Custard: 1½ cups milk, ¾ pound firm tofu, ¾ teaspoon ground turmeric, ¾ teaspoon salt. Reduce baking time.

Yield: 6 to 8 servings

Cheese & Broccoli Soufflé

A delicious complete-protein soufflé that never falls and never fails to please. Very filling and satisfying.

Batter:
1   cup milk
½   cup unbleached white flour
      or whole wheat flour
¼   teaspoon baking powder
¼   cup grated Parmesan cheese
1   cup ricotta cheese or low fat
      cottage cheese
¾   cup firm tofu, crumbled and drained
1   teaspoon prepared sharp mustard
⅛   teaspoon cayenne pepper or to taste

½   teaspoon ground turmeric
¾   teaspoon salt
1   tablespoon vegetable oil
      Black pepper to taste
Filling:
1   10-ounce package frozen chopped
      broccoli, thawed and drained
1   cup shredded sharp Cheddar cheese
¾   cup firm tofu, crumbled and drained

● Process all batter ingredients in a blender or food processor until smooth. Set aside.
● Combine filling ingredients in a large bowl. Add batter and mix well. Spread soufflé mixture into a shallow soufflé dish, 10-inch quiche dish or a deep 9-inch pie plate. ● Bake at 350° F. for 35 to 45 minutes until the top is nicely browned. Let stand 15 minutes before serving.

Note: Other frozen chopped vegetables, such as asparagus or spinach, can be substituted for the broccoli. The soufflé can also be made without vegetables.

Yield: 6 servings

Quiche Crust

Use this flaky crust for quiches or any vegetable pie.

1½ cups unbleached white flour
½   teaspoon salt

½   cup cold butter
⅓   cup (scant) ice water

● Sift flour and salt together. Slice the butter into ¼-inch slices and drop into flour. Using a pastry blender or two knives, cut the butter into the flour until it resembles coarse cornmeal.
● Sprinkle ice water into the mixture and stir it quickly with a fork just until the dough holds together. Form into a ball and cover with plastic wrap. Chill for 2 hours. ● Roll the dough on a lightly floured surface to form a circle that is about 2½ inches larger than your pan. (For the quiche recipes in this book, use a small 9-inch quiche pan or a 9-inch pie plate.) Position pastry in the center of your pan and press in evenly. Trim dough around the edge to be about ¼ inch wider than the pan. Crimp the edges of dough with a pastry crimper or your fingers. Chill for 30 minutes. ● Prick the bottom of the crust, then line the inside of the pastry with aluminum foil. Fill the foil with dried beans. (Save the beans for this purpose again, but do not try to cook them for eating.) Bake at 450° F. for about 8 minutes. Remove foil with beans and bake for 3 to 5 more minutes until the bottom of the pastry shell is a light golden color. Remove from oven and let cool on a wire rack before filling.

Yield: pastry for one 9-inch quiche

Mushroom Broccoli Quiche

This delicious and popular quiche can be enjoyed year-round.

1	9-inch Quiche Crust
1	medium-sized onion, chopped
2	tablespoons vegetable oil
12	medium-sized fresh mushrooms, sliced
½	teaspoon crumbled dry basil
½	teaspoon dry parsley flakes or
	1½ teaspoons chopped fresh parsley
	Salt and pepper to taste
1	cup shredded Swiss, Monterey Jack or
	Cheddar cheese

Custard:

1¼	cups ricotta cheese, at room temperature
¼	cup half and half cream or milk
¼	cup dry egg replacer
½	cup finely chopped broccoli flowerets
	Freshly ground nutmeg
	Salt to taste
	Cayenne pepper to taste

Garnish:

Additional sliced fresh mushrooms
Paprika

● Prepare Quiche Crust and set aside to cool. ● Sauté onion in vegetable oil until soft. Add mushrooms, basil, parsley, salt and pepper. Sauté until all excess liquid evaporates. Set aside to cool. ● Shred cheese and set aside. ● For the custard, combine ricotta cheese, half and half cream or milk and dry egg replacer in a mixing bowl. Beat until smooth. Stir in broccoli, nutmeg, salt and cayenne pepper. ● Spread sautéed vegetables in the bottom of the Quiche Crust. Sprinkle with shredded cheese. Top with the custard mixture. Spread custard over the cheese by mounding it in the center of the quiche and gently spreading it to the outer edges of the crust. Garnish with sliced mushrooms and a sprinkling of paprika. ● Bake at 400° F. for 20 minutes. Turn off oven heat and leave quiche in the oven for another 20 minutes. The top should puff up slightly and turn a golden brown. Remove from oven and let cool for 10 minutes before serving. Cut into wedges. Can be served hot or at room temperature.

Yield: 4 to 6 servings

Asparagus Pimento Quiche

This quiche combines the spring-like flavor of asparagus and the refreshing taste of pimento with a colorful custard.

1	9-inch Quiche Crust
14	fresh asparagus spears or 1 10-ounce package frozen asparagus
4	ounces whole pimentos, cut into 1-inch slices
3	tablespoons dairy sour cream
1⅓	cups shredded Swiss or Muenster cheese Salt and pepper to taste

Custard:

1¼	cup ricotta cheese, at room temperature
¼	cup half and half cream or milk
¼	cup dry egg replacer
3	tablespoons chopped pimentos
¼	teaspoon salt Cayenne pepper to taste

Garnish:

2	ounces sliced pimentos, cut into 1½-inch strips Paprika

● Prepare Quiche Crust and set aside to cool. ● Wash and trim fresh asparagus. Cook covered in ¼ cup boiling water over medium heat for about 6 minutes or until just tender. Drain well and pat dry with paper towels when cool enough to handle. Cut into 1-inch pieces. If using frozen asparagus, cook covered in ¼ cup boiling water for 5 minutes or until just tender. Drain well and pat dry when cooled. Set aside. ● Drain pimentos on paper towels. Combine with asparagus in a bowl. Add sour cream, ⅓ cup of the shredded cheese, salt and pepper. Spread this mixture in the bottom of the Quiche Crust. ● Sprinkle remaining 1 cup of cheese over the asparagus mixture. Combine custard ingredients and mix well. Layer the custard over the cheese by mounding it in the center of the quiche and gently spreading it to the outer edges of the crust. Garnish with sliced pimentos and a sprinkling of paprika. ● Bake at 400° F. for 20 minutes. Turn off oven heat and leave quiche in the oven for another 20 minutes. The top should puff slightly and turn a golden brown. Remove from oven and let cool 10 minutes before serving. Cut into wedges. Can be served hot or at room temperature.

Yield: 4 to 6 servings

Spinach Artichoke Quiche

You will appreciate the artful combination of the inimitable artichoke topped with a splendid spinach and cream cheese mixture, tangy Cheddar cheese, and our light ricotta custard.

1	9-inch Quiche Crust
1	9-ounce package frozen artichoke hearts
1¼	cups shredded sharp Cheddar cheese
	Salt and pepper
½	teaspoon crumbled dry oregano
1	pound fresh spinach, chopped or 1 10-ounce package chopped spinach
1	3-ounce package cream cheese, at room temperature
1	garlic clove, crushed

Freshly ground nutmeg
Custard:

1¼	cups ricotta cheese, at room temperature
¼	cup half and half cream or milk
¼	cup dry egg replacer
	Freshly ground nutmeg
	Salt and pepper

Garnish:

Artichoke hearts (reserved)
Paprika

● Prepare Quiche Crust and set aside to cool. ● Cook frozen artichoke hearts in a covered pan in ¼ cup boiling water for 5 minutes. Drain well and cool for easy handling. Squeeze excess water from hearts. Cut into quarters and reserve 8 quarters for the garnish. ● Sprinkle ¼ cup of the Cheddar cheese into the bottom of the pie crust. Arrange artichoke hearts over cheese. Sprinkle with salt, pepper and oregano. ● Cook fresh spinach in a covered pan in ¼ cup boiling water until spinach is limp. Drain well. If using frozen spinach, just thaw spinach and squeeze excess water out with your hands. ● Combine spinach with cream cheese, garlic and nutmeg. Mix well and spread over the artichokes. Top with the remaining 1 cup of Cheddar cheese. ● Combine custard ingredients. Spread custard over the cheese by mounding it in the center of the quiche and gently spreading it to the outer edges of the crust. Garnish with reserved artichoke hearts and a sprinkling of paprika. ● Bake at 400° F. for 20 minutes. Turn off oven heat and leave quiche in the oven for another 20 minutes. The top should puff up slightly and turn a golden brown. Remove from oven and let cool for 10 minutes before serving. Cut into wedges. Can be served hot or at room temperature.

Yield: 4 to 6 servings

Eggless Creations

Red & Green Pepper Quiche

A colorful quiche with an Italian flair.

1	9-inch Quiche Crust
1	medium-sized onion, chopped
2	tablespoons olive oil
1	small red bell pepper, sliced into 1-inch strips
1	small green bell pepper cut into 1-inch strips
¼	teaspoon crumbled dry oregano
¼	teaspoon crumbled dry basil
	Salt and pepper to taste
8	pimento-stuffed green olives, sliced
8	pitted black olives, sliced
5	tablespoons grated Parmesan cheese

2	tablespoons unbleached white flour or whole wheat flour
1	cup shredded mozzarella cheese, packed

Custard:

1¼	cups ricotta cheese, at room temperature
¼	cup half and half cream or milk
¼	cup dry egg replacer
¼	cup Parmesan cheese
3	teaspoons capers, drained
	Salt and pepper to taste

Garnish:

Sliced black and green olives
Paprika

● Prepare Quiche Crust and set aside to cool. ● Sauté onions in vegetable oil until soft. Add red and green bell peppers, oregano, basil, salt and pepper. Sauté until bell peppers are limp, about 10 minutes. Add green and black sliced olives, 2 tablespoons of the Parmesan cheese, and flour. Stir well and cook for 1 minute. Set aside to cool. Combine remaining 3 tablespoons Parmesan cheese with mozzarella cheese. Set aside. ● Mix custard ingredients together in a bowl. When sautéed vegetables have cooled, spread them in the bottom of the Quiche Crust. Sprinkle with the mixed cheeses and top with custard mixture. Spread the custard over the cheese by mounding it in the center of the quiche and gently spreading it to the outer edges of the crust. Garnish with olives and a sprinkling of paprika. ● Bake at 400° F. for 20 minutes. Turn off oven heat and leave quiche in the oven for another 20 minutes. The top should puff up slightly and turn a golden brown. Remove from oven and let cool for 10 minutes before serving. Cut into wedges. Can be served hot or at room temperature.

Yield: 4 to 6 servings

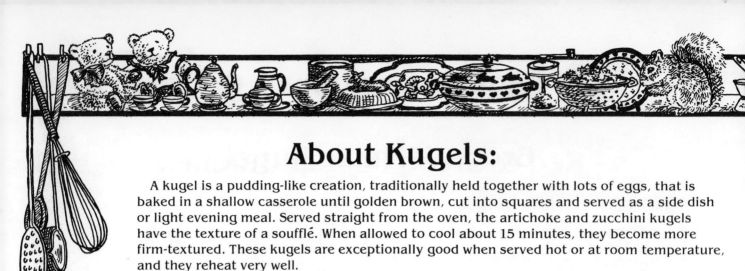

About Kugels:

A kugel is a pudding-like creation, traditionally held together with lots of eggs, that is baked in a shallow casserole until golden brown, cut into squares and served as a side dish or light evening meal. Served straight from the oven, the artichoke and zucchini kugels have the texture of a soufflé. When allowed to cool about 15 minutes, they become more firm-textured. These kugels are exceptionally good when served hot or at room temperature, and they reheat very well.

Zucchini Kugel

The abundance of zucchini and the ease of preparation make this dish a year-round favorite.

4 cups shredded zucchini	1½ cups crushed crackers
1 medium-sized onion, chopped	Salt and freshly ground black pepper to taste
3 tablespoons vegetable oil	
1½ cups shredded Swiss cheese	

● Set shredded zucchini aside in a colander for one hour. Drain, squeezing out excess liquid and place in a large bowl. ● Sauté onion in 1 tablespoon of the vegetable oil until golden. Add onion to zucchini along with 1 cup of the cheese. ● Measure out 1¼ cups of the crushed crackers and add to zucchini along with remaining 2 tablespoons vegetable oil, salt and black pepper. (The amount of salt needed will depend upon the salt content of the crackers you use.) Mix well. ● Turn into an oiled 8x8-inch baking pan. Combine remaining ½ cup of cheese and ¼ cup crushed crackers. Sprinkle over top. ● Bake at 350° F. for 35 minutes until lightly browned. Let stand for 5 minutes before serving.

Yield: 6 servings

Artichoke Kugel

This kugel is enhanced by the deep flavor of marinated artichokes along with tofu, scallions and sharp Cheddar cheese.

2 6-ounce jars marinated artichoke hearts	2 tablespoons vegetable oil
1½ cups water	12 ounces tofu, mashed and drained
4 cups oyster-style crackers or saltines broken into 1-inch pieces	1½ cups shredded Cheddar cheese
¾ cup thinly sliced scallions	Freshly ground black pepper

● Drain artichokes, saving marinade. Place marinade in a large bowl with water and crackers. Let crackers stand for 10 to 15 minutes until liquid is absorbed. Stir occasionally to keep crackers coated. ● Sauté scallions in 1 tablespoon of the vegetable oil. Add scallions to crackers along with tofu, cheese, black pepper to taste and remaining 1 tablespoon of vegetable oil. Mix thoroughly, crushing any crackers that are not soft. Coarsely chop artichokes and stir into crackers. ● Turn into an oiled 8x8-inch baking pan. Bake at 350° F. for 40 minutes until lightly browned.

Yield: 8 servings

Broccoli Matzo Kugel

A unique kugel that is easy to make and is sure to be enjoyed.

5	large matzos or 4 cups sesame crackers	1	cup shredded sharp Cheddar cheese
2	cups boiling water	2	carrots, shredded
3	vegetable bouillon cubes	1	cup crumbled firm tofu, drained
3	medium-sized onions, diced		Salt and black pepper
2	cups chopped broccoli flowerets and small stalks	1	teaspoon poppy or sesame seeds (optional)
5	tablespoons vegetable oil		

● Break matzos or crackers into 2-inch pieces. If using small crackers, leave whole. Combine water and bouillon cubes, letting cubes dissolve, and pour over crackers. Mix well and let stand 5 minutes. ● Saute onion with broccoli in the vegetable oil until onions are soft. Add to crackers along with cheese, carrots, tofu, salt and black pepper to taste (see note). ● Turn into an oiled 8x8-inch pan. Sprinkle seeds over top. Bake at 350° F. for 50 to 55 minutes until golden. Let stand for 15 minutes before serving.

Note: Adjust salt amount depending upon the type of crackers you use.

Yield: 8 main servings

Pasta Kugel

This rich and slightly sweet specialty is a hit at any meal, buffet or party.

1	pound uncooked elbow or spiral macaroni, cooked al dente	½	cup unsalted butter, melted
2	pints dairy sour cream	2	tablespoons vanilla extract
2	pounds large curd cottage cheese	1	cup raisins
1	cup sugar		Cornflake crumbs
			Ground cinnamon
		2	tablespoons butter

● Drain pasta when cooked. ● Combine sour cream, cottage cheese, sugar, melted butter, vanilla extract and raisins. Stir into pasta. ● Butter a 10x15-inch baking pan and sprinkle a thin coating of cornflake crumbs on the bottom. Pour in macaroni mixture. Top with a sprinkle of cinnamon, more cornflakes crumbs, then a little more cinnamon. Dot with 2 tablespoons butter. ● Bake at 350° F. for 1 hour or until set and golden brown on top.

Yield: 12 servings

133

Zucchini Frittata

A frittata is an Italian-style omelet in which the filling ingredients are mixed into the batter before cooking. Our handsome rendition has a layer of sliced zucchini as a base, a flavorful batter and filling laced with chopped spinach, and a topping of seasoned fresh tomatoes.

Batter:
½	cup milk
½	cup unbleached white flour
¼	teaspoon baking powder
¼	cup grated Parmesan cheese
1	cup ricotta cheese or low fat cottage cheese
¾	cup crumbled tofu, drained
¼	teaspoon crumbled dry oregano
¼	teaspoon crumbled dry basil
½	teaspoon ground turmeric
¾	teaspoon salt
1	tablespoon vegetable oil
	Black pepper to taste

Filling:
3	6-inch zucchini, cut into ¼-inch slices
2	to 3 tablespoons vegetable oil
	Salt and pepper
	Garlic powder
1	10-ounce package frozen chopped spinach, thawed and drained or 1 pound fresh spinach, steamed and drained
½	cup shredded mozzarella cheese
½	cup shredded colby or sharp Cheddar cheese
¾	cup crumbled tofu, drained

Topping:
3	medium-sized tomatoes, sliced
	Salt and pepper
¼	teaspoon crumbled dry marjoram or basil
	Grated Parmesan cheese

● Process all batter ingredients together in a blender or food processor until smooth. Set aside. Lightly sauté zucchini slices in vegetable oil until golden. Arrange zucchini in circles over the bottom and up the sides of a round shallow casserole or large (10- to 11-inch) quiche dish. Season with a light sprinkling of salt, pepper and garlic powder. ● Squeeze spinach between your hands to press out excess liquid. Combine spinach in a large bowl with cheeses and tofu. Add puréed batter ingredients and mix well. ● Spoon mixture over zucchini carefully so as not to disturb slices. Top with sliced tomatoes. Sprinkle with salt, pepper, marjoram or basil, and Parmesan cheese. ● Bake at 375° F. for 45 minutes. Remove from oven and let stand for 5 to 10 minutes. Cut into wedges and serve.

Yield: 6 servings

Tofu Rancheros

For a real south-of-the-border flavor, try this hearty dish which doubles as a filling for tacos or tortillas.

1	small onion, chopped
½	large green bell pepper, chopped
6	medium-sized fresh mushrooms, sliced
2	tablespoons vegetable oil
8	vegetarian sausages, sliced (optional)
1	pound firm tofu, crumbled and drained
½	teaspoon ground turmeric

1	teaspoon salt
1	to 2 teaspoons chili powder
1	cup cooked kidney beans, drained
¼	to ½ cup marinara or tomato sauce
8	cherry tomatoes, halved or 1 large tomato, cut into wedges

● Sauté onion, green pepper and mushrooms in vegetable oil for 3 minutes. Add vegetarian sausage and sauté 1 minute. ● Mix in tofu and all remaining ingredients except fresh tomatoes. Cook over medium heat, stirring occasionally, until hot. Add tomatoes. Cover and cook 2 minutes until tomatoes are heated through.

Yield: 4 servings

Scrambled Tofu

A fast and reliable standby that makes an appealing high-protein meal. Scrambled tofu lends itself to many variations and is delicious when served in a pita bread or on toast.

3	tablespoons butter
½	teaspoon turmeric
2	tablespoons minced fresh onion or
	¾ teaspoon onion powder
12	ounces firm tofu, coarsely crumbled
	and drained
	Salt and black pepper to taste

Optionals:

¼	cup sliced fresh mushrooms
¼	cup diced green bell pepper
¼	cup sliced vegetarian sausage
	or vegetarian hot dog
2	tablespoons cream cheese
¼	cup shredded Cheddar cheese

● Melt butter in a skillet over medium heat. Stir in turmeric. Add onion and your choice of mushrooms, bell pepper and vegetarian sausage or hot dog. Saute 3 minutes, stirring occasionally. ● Add tofu and stir gently until well mixed and heated through. Add cream cheese and / or Cheddar cheese if desired. Cook and stir until cheese is melted. Season with salt and black pepper.

Note: You can experiment with a variety of items to be added to the Scrambled Tofu such as chopped broccoli, shredded zucchini, seasoned beans, etc. The addition of cream cheese gives the tofu a creamy texture.

Yield: 2 servings

Tofu Indian-Style

Scrambled tofu, potatoes and vegetables are simmered in piquant Indian spices to make this an outstanding brunch or supper dish.

2	medium-sized potatoes
1	medium-sized onion, chopped
1	garlic clove, crushed
¼	cup vegetable oil
1	cup chopped fresh tomato
¼	teaspoon ground turmeric

¼	teaspoon ground cumin
¼	teaspoon ground coriander
1½	teaspoons salt
¼	teaspoon cayenne pepper (optional)
1½	cups water
2	cups chopped cauliflower
¾	cup frozen peas
1	pound firm tofu, crumbled and drained

● Peel potatoes, if desired, and cut into ½-inch cubes. Place in a bowl of cold water to prevent discoloration. ● In a large skillet, saute onion and garlic in vegetable oil until onion starts to turn light brown. Add tomato, turmeric, cumin, coriander, salt and cayenne pepper. Cook for 3 minutes, stirring constantly. ● Drain potatoes and add to skillet along with water. Cover and cook over medium heat for 10 minutes. Add cauliflower, stir well, and cook covered for 10 more minutes. ● Mix in peas and tofu. Reduce heat and cook uncovered for 10 minutes, stirring occasionally.

Yield: 4 servings

Basic Omelet

Here tofu is transformed into a remarkable eggless omelet. Low in cholesterol and easy to prepare, this omelet is delicious with any of our tasty fillings.

6 **ounces firm tofu (1 cup crumbled), well drained**	**Dash of black pepper**
¼ **cup milk**	**¹/₈** **teaspoon (scant) ground turmeric**
¹/₈ **teaspoon (scant) salt**	**½** **tablespoon butter**

● Process all ingredients except butter in a blender until smooth. ● Preheat oven broiler. ● Melt butter in a 7- or 8-inch non-stick skillet or omelet pan. Pour in tofu batter and spread evenly with a spatula. Cook, without stirring, over medium heat for a few minutes until the edges are set but not browned. The batter will bubble up as excess liquid evaporates. ● Remove from burner and place under preheated broiler for 2 to 3 minutes until the top is set and has just a hint of brown. ● Remove from broiler and add filling, if desired, to one half of the omelet. Using a spatula, carefully fold other half of omelet over the filling. The omelet is delicate, and if it breaks a little, just smooth it with your spatula. Spread the top with butter if desired. ● Place under broiler again for 1 to 2 minutes until golden brown. Serve at once.

Yield: 1 serving

Spinach & Cheese Omelet

The fresh taste of mushrooms combined with your favorite melted cheese makes a quick and tempting omelet filling.

1 **Basic Omelet**	**¹/₃** **to ½ cup torn fresh spinach leaves**
Pinch of crumbled dry basil	**¹/₃** **to ½ cup shredded cheese**
Pinch of crumbled dry thyme	

● Prepare Basic Omelet as directed, adding basil and thyme to the batter during blending for additional flavor. ● Cook omelet according to Basic Omelet instructions, using spinach and cheese for the filling.

Yield: 1 serving

Western Omelet

For a satisfying meal, stuff an omelet with this exciting assortment of cooked potatoes and vegetables sparked with the flavor of vegetarian sausages.

2 tablespoons chopped onion	2 tablespoons chopped fresh mushrooms
½ tablespoon butter or vegetable oil	1 vegetarian sausage, sliced (optional)
2 tablespoons diced cooked potato	Pinch of salt and black pepper
2 tablespoons chopped green or red bell pepper	1 Basic Omelet
	Shredded cheese for top (optional)

● Sauté onion in butter or vegetable oil until softened. Add potato, bell pepper, mushrooms and sausage. Saute briefly. Season lightly with salt and pepper. ● Prepare omelet according to Basic Omelet instructions, using sauteed vegetables for the filling. After folding omelet over filling, sprinkle shredded cheese over top if desired before broiling.

Yield: 1 serving

Broccoli & Mushroom Omelet

Here is a wonderful full-flavored omelet for serving at breakfast, lunch or supper.

¼ cup chopped onion	Dash of garlic powder
¼ cup chopped broccoli flowerets	1 Basic Omelet
1 tablespoon butter or vegetable oil	1 teaspoon tamari
¼ cup chopped fresh mushrooms	Pinch of crumbled dry tarragon
Salt and pepper	¼ cup shredded cheese (optional)

● Sauté onion and broccoli in butter or vegetable oil until softened. Add mushrooms and sauté briefly. Season lightly with salt, pepper and garlic powder. ● Prepare Basic Omelet batter, adding tamari to batter during blending for additional seasoning. Stir in tarragon after blending. ● Cook according to Basic Omelet instructions, using sautéed vegetables and shredded cheese for the filling.

Yield: 1 serving

Glossary

Agar: Agar is made from seaweed and can often be used in place of commercial gelatin. It can be purchased in health food stores, where it is sold in three forms: flakes, granules and in a solid bar called kanten. The three different types of agar all have different jelling properties and should not be used interchangeably without adjusting the proportions of liquid ingredients in any given recipe. The recipes in this book specify agar flakes.

Bulgar: Bulgar, sometimes spelled bulghur, is cracked, dried wheat that has been partially cooked. It comes in three sizes: fine, medium and coarse. Bulgar can be purchased at health food stores, groceries specializing in Greek or Mid-Eastern foods, and in many supermarkets.

Cardamom: This aromatic spice lends its flavor to many Indian recipes. Cardamom is sold either whole in the pod or ground. If a recipe calls for whole cardamom or crushed cardamom seeds, it is necessary to open the pods and remove the seeds before using them.

Carob (St. John's bread): The pods of the carob tree are ground to make carob powder. While some people enjoy carob in its own right, others use it as a substitute for chocolate.

Cellophane noodles: These thread-like noodles are made from mung beans and can be found in Oriental grocery stores and some supermarkets.

Cheese: Although everyone is familiar with at least a few of the many varieties of cheese available today, it is important to note that in the manufacturing of cheese there are basically two types of coagulants used: one is rennet, which is obtained from the lining of a calf's stomach, and the other is vegetarian. Strictly vegetarian cheese is rennetless. Many large cheese manufacturers use vegetarian microbial enzymes rather than rennet as a coagulant, although their products may not be labeled "rennetless" and their source of enzymes may not be specified (animal or microbial). The different types of cheese featured in *Classics & Creations* can be obtained in rennetless form in many locations, and most cheese

manufacturers will identify which of their products are rennetless upon inquiry. Also, most health food stores carry some rennetless cheese.

Coriander (Cilantro): Fresh coriander, sometimes called Chinese parsley, is used in many Indian and South American recipes and may be purchased wherever Indian or Latin American foods are sold. Dried coriander seeds are available both whole and ground in the spice section of supermarkets, but they are not a substitute for the fresh leaves.

Cumin: This uniquely-flavored spice is used throughout the Middle-East, India and South America, either as whole seeds or in ground form. It can almost always be found on the supermarket shelf.

Dulse: Dulse is a sea vegetable that is very high in iodine and other minerals. It is available in dried form in most health food stores and in some supermarkets.

Egg replacer: There are several ways to replace eggs in cooking and baking, and in this book we have used three popular egg replacers: tofu, lecithin and dry egg replacer. Where tofu or lecithin are used, our recipes include them specifically as ingredients. Dry egg replacer is available commercially, and the brand that we have used most often is called Ener-G, available from Ener-G Foods, Inc., P.O. Box 24723, Seattle, WA 98124 or from your health food store. When using dry egg replacer in these recipes, use only the amounts of liquid as given in the recipe and do not reconstitute with additional water.

Enoki mushrooms: These small, fresh mushrooms are sold in Oriental grocery stores. Before using them, always trim off the lower part of the stems.

Ginger root: The fresh root of the ginger plant is peeled before being grated, diced or sliced. Use fresh ginger wherever it is called for rather than the powdered form which is commonly used only for baking. Fresh ginger is now available in most supermarkets as well as Oriental and Latin American food stores.

Kasha: Kasha (roasted, cracked buckwheat kernels) is a highly nutritious grain with a distinctive, hearty flavor.

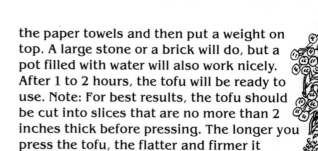

Lecithin: Lecithin, derived from soybeans, comes in both liquid and granular forms. It is used as an emulsifier in cooking and may also be used as a substitute for eggs in some recipes. It is rich in polyunsaturated fats and has no cholesterol. It can be purchased in health food stores.

Matzo: Matzo is unleavened bread which is made in large squares and closely resembles crackers both in flavor and texture. It is always found in stores which carry Jewish foods and sometimes may be found in supermarkets.

Matzo meal: Matzo meal is the crumb form of matzo. In many recipes, cracker crumbs may be substituted for matzo meal.

Miso: Miso is fermented soybean paste and is high in protein. It comes in many different varieties (red, white and yellow, each bearing different names) and is available in Japanese grocery stores and most health food stores. Lighter miso tend to be sweeter than the darker ones, which are quite salty. Miso makes a flavorful soup broth and may be added to stews or sauces. Miso should never be boiled.

Nori: Nori is a dry sea vegetable which is sold in thin sheets and is very high in protein, vitamins and minerals. Nori is commonly available both toasted and untoasted in Oriental food stores or some health food stores.

Nutritional yeast: These protein-rich yellow flakes are high in B vitamins and impart a rich, meaty taste to gravies or stews. Nutritional yeast is sold in packages or in bulk in health food stores; and we recommend that when buying nutritional yeast, you ask for the best-tasting brand, as flavors vary. Do not confuse nutritional yeast with yeast used for baking or with brewer's yeast which, although nutritionally similar, is often bitter.

Pine nuts: These small, oval nuts have a distinctive flavor and are an excellent source of protein. They are quite rich, so a little goes a long way.

Pressed tofu: (see tofu.) To press tofu, cover a large flat plate or smooth surface with several layers of newspapers. Cover paper with a few layers of paper towels. Place the tofu on the paper towels, cover with a few more layers of paper towels, then more newspaper. Place a flat plate on top of the paper towels and then put a weight on top. A large stone or a brick will do, but a pot filled with water will also work nicely. After 1 to 2 hours, the tofu will be ready to use. Note: For best results, the tofu should be cut into slices that are no more than 2 inches thick before pressing. The longer you press the tofu, the flatter and firmer it becomes.

Sesame oil: Light sesame oil is made from raw sesame seeds and can be used like most oils. Oriental sesame oil, made from the roasted seeds, is used in small quantities as a flavoring and gives Chinese food a distinctive taste. This dark, aromatic oil can be purchased in Oriental food stores and in some supermarkets.

Sour salt: Sour salt, which is another name for citric acid, is usually found in the canning section of the supermarket. Citric acid is added to low-acid fruits before they are processed and is also added to fruits before they are frozen to preserve their color.

Sprouts: Seeds, grains or beans showing tiny shoots at the beginning of their growth are called sprouts. At one time they could be bought only in health food stores, however it is not unusual today to find a variety of fresh sprouts in supermarkets. If you wish to try growing sprouts at home, the process is quite simple and takes only a few days. Care should be taken to buy only those seeds, beans or grains which have not been chemically treated in any way and are sold for food, not seed. The simplest method of sprouting is to soak the seeds, beans or grains overnight in warm water, using 1 part seeds, beans or grains to 4 parts water. In the morning, drain them and then rinse them thoroughly with warm water. Place them in a clean glass jar and cover with cheese cloth for coarse grains or beans, or a piece of nylon stocking for finer seeds. A fine wire mesh strainer also works well. Rinse the sprouts in warm water a few times a day, draining them thoroughly each time, and continue this rinsing process for 3 to 4 days, at which time the sprouts should be ready to eat. Also, the seeds, beans or grains should be kept out of direct sunlight while they are being sprouted and then should be put in the sun for a day until they develop chlorophyll and turn green.

Tamari: Tamari is an aged, fermented soy sauce with a rich, robust taste. It is superior to ordinary soy sauce and we recommend it in our recipes. Tamari is made from wheat and soybeans but is available wheat-free and, for people who wish to restrict their salt, in low-salt varieties. It can be purchased in health food stores.

Tahini: Tahini is made from ground, hulled sesame seeds. It is rich in protein and calcium and is similar in texture to thin, smooth peanut butter. Tahini has a high oil content and sometimes separates into two layers with a stiff paste on the bottom and oil on the top. If this happens, process the tahini in a blender or a food processor until it becomes homogenized again.

Textured vegetable protein (TVP): TVP is dehydrated plant protein. Although each brand has its own instructions for rehydration, our recipes use dry TVP and include all liquids necessary. TVP may be purchased flavored or unflavored.

Tofu: Tofu, which is also known as bean curd or soy cheese, is a versatile all-purpose food. Tofu is an excellent source of protein; it is high in calcium, low in calories, has no cholesterol and is easy to digest. Tofu, by itself, is bland and will absorb the flavors of the foods with which it is cooked. Tofu is sold in soft or firm cakes, and because the water content of each differs, it is important to use the type specified. Tofu may be purchased at health food stores and in some supermarkets. To be good, tofu has to be fresh. Tofu should be covered with cold water and stored in the refrigerator. To keep tofu fresh, change the water every day. (See pressed tofu.)

Tempeh: Tempeh is a fermented food made from soybeans. It is easy to digest and very rich in vitamins and minerals, especially B-12. Tempeh can be added to soups, stews, sandwiches and casseroles. It can also be fried, baked or broiled. Tempeh is a wonderful source of protein, 4 ounces supplying 22 grams.

Turmeric: Turmeric is an aromatic herb which is used both for flavor and color in Indian food. Because of its rich, yellow color, we use it in many of our tofu recipes.

Vegeburger: Canned vegetarian burger is available in health food stores.

Vegetable bouillon: Most health food stores sell at least one form of vegetable bouillon, either in powder, cubes or paste. When using bouillon, adjust the salt after all the ingredients are added, as the sodium content of various bouillons differs.

Vegetarian hot dogs and sausages: Canned hot dogs and sausages, prepared without any animal products, are carried by most health food stores.

 # Glossary

Index

Index

Index

Recipes